WHEN THE CREW MATTER MOST

Also by Erroll Bruce

DEEP-SEA SAILING
CHALLENGE TO POSEIDON

1   The sloop *Belmore* sets out from Portsmouth

WHEN THE CREW MATTER MOST

an ocean-racing story

ERROLL BRUCE

STANLEY PAUL
London

STANLEY PAUL & CO. LTD

178-202 Great Portland Street, London, W.1

AN IMPRINT OF THE HUTCHINSON GROUP

London Melbourne Sydney
Auckland Bombay Toronto
Johannesburg New York

First published 1961

*This book has been set in Bembo type face. It has
been printed in Great Britain by The Anchor Press,
Ltd., in Tiptree, Essex, on Antique Wove paper and
bound by Taylor Garnett Evans & Co., Ltd., in
Watford, Herts*

Contents

Illustrations

The sketches were drawn on board *Belmore* by Roy Mullender.

Figs. 1, 2, and 4 are reproduced from the daily weather reports of the British Meteorological Office by permission of H.M. Stationary Office.

Fig. 3 is reproduced from an Admiralty synoptic chart by permission of the Admiralty.

Plate No. 1 is reproduced by courtesy of Portsmouth and Sunderland Newspapers Ltd.

Plates Nos. 8, 9, 10, 12, 13, 14, 15, 16, 17, 18, 19 by courtesy of the Bermuda News Bureau.

I

Outward Bound

ON THE last day of April 1960 the eleven-ton yacht *Belmore*
lay alongside the captain's gangway of H.M.S. *Vernon*, a naval
shore establishment at Portsmouth. She was in the heart of the
Royal Navy, to which all her crew belonged, and although her
venture could have no official naval support, individuals of the
Royal Navy were gathered to give a warm send-off to its six
members who were to represent them in an exacting task.

It was a typical naval ceremony adapted to a Saturday
afternoon, which is the time normally reserved for sport. The
crew of *Belmore* lined their deck, dressed in blue trousers,
white high-necked jerseys, with blue-white-and-red woollen
caps; the chaplain in his robes said a few simple prayers of
dedication and blessing; an admiral in naval uniform read a
passage from the Bible; the gathering of families and fellow
yachtsmen sang a hymn. Then slowly the little yacht, scrubbed
and polished as for a christening, moved out of the creek with
the whisper of hushed wind in her sails. At the creek entrance
lay to port the Union Jacks of one trio of tethered warships
towering above her, while to starboard the White Ensigns of
another group were level with her yard-arm, from which
fluttered a hoist of her own small flags; they signalled the
naval message 'Intend to proceed in execution of previous
orders'.

Now these were the orders that I had been given as skipper
of *Belmore* for her Atlantic task; they were signed by Admiral

Sir Manley Power, elected Commodore of the Royal Naval Sailing Association:

1. You are hereby directed to take the yacht *Belmore* under your command, on behalf of the Royal Naval Sailing Association, to which she has been loaned by T. W. M. Steele, Esq.

2. Your objects are the winning of the Bermuda race, organized by the Cruising Club of America, and the Transatlantic race, organized by the Royal Swedish Yacht Club. You are to use every endeavour to achieve these objects within the rules set by these clubs, and guided by the standards of seamanship and sportsmanship traditionally set by the Royal Naval Sailing Association. Where the requirements of the two races might conflict, you are to use your discretion about which will bring most credit to the Royal Naval Sailing Association.

3. You are to plan the movements of the yacht at your discretion, entering her in any other races in the name of the Royal Naval Sailing Association. You may enter the waters of any country necessary, taking care to comply with the requirements of that country.

4. You are to endeavour to bring the yacht back to Portsmouth in time for return to her owner by 15th August.

Such were my orders, with the purpose of the venture as clear as was the discretion allowed in executing them. *Belmore* turned up-harbour to wait, while those who had gathered to pray with her company manned their own vesels and sailed to escort her out of harbour.

It was a gallant sight for us as we beat to windward past the fleet of yachts and boats, letting fly our vast genoa to flutter a reply to the cheers of each one in turn. There was our Commodore, stately in his yacht *Norvessa*; then each one of the flag officers to support him: Admiral Sir Ballin Robertshaw, Vice-Commodore, who had my wife in his crew of the *Valiant Maid*; Commander Alan Miller, R.N.V.R., in his *Nantucket*, a close cousin of the American *Finisterre*, which was to be one of our special rivals; then cleaving gracefully through the water at speed came Captain Morgan Giles' *Clarion*, wearing at the masthead his rear-commodore's flag and at the stem-head my younger daughter Errollyn. Flying the club burgee was the large *Marabu*, who had herself made a similar voyage eight years before; there was also *Meon Maid*, sister to *Belmore*, *Seehexe*, whalers, dinghies, and several more yachts, which all formed our escort, as we beat towards Spithead. Last to leave us was an admiral's barge, from which my younger son Peter, on leave from Dartmouth College, handed back the camera with which he had photographed our departure.

The crew of *Belmore* worked smoothly as we tacked out of harbour; we had already practised onboard the yacht during several weekend sails, including an Easter cruise across the Channel in company with *Danegeld* from Cowes, who was to join with us for the whole Atlantic venture, representing the Island Sailing Club.

We had also sailed a couple of day-passage races, from Lymington to Poole one day, and the return passage the next. These races had attracted a good number of fine ocean-racing and cruising yachts, for most of whom it was the first outing of the season. In *Belmore* we took each race as a serious exercise for the whole crew to concentrate on their racing duties for several hours without pausing, and, throughout, the six of us had remained closed up at full racing stations.

For this the skipper was normally at the tiller, but always ready to take over at a moment's notice was Peter Paffard, the tactician and navigator; his post at racing stations was normally in the main hatch, a position sacred to skipper and navigator. From there he could see all around, and had the chart-table and navigational instruments immediately beneath him. When manœuvring for the start of a race the navigator would check each item of the race instructions, confirm the starting line, operate the starting watch, and keep a special eye on yachts abaft the beam. At the skipper's order 'Ready about', the navigator would report all clear astern, or any danger of collision that might arise from the change in course. He would report the minutes left before the starting-gun, besides a count down in seconds for the last half-minute; at any moment in between he would have to be able to answer such questions as 'time to go', 'course after the start', 'relative wind if I'm steering 330', 'what is the blue yacht and what does she rate?'

Should any other yacht approach, however simple the rule of the road, he would confirm the rights with a simple report such as 'You have the right over 625' or 'You give way to the blue yawl'. If the rights were uncertain he would ask: 'Have you the right over 1118?'

Whenever at racing stations the navigator had to know the position of the yacht, have on the tip of his tongue the depth when in shallow water, all that could be discovered about the tides and currents, the best theoretical course to steer at any moment, and every detail of the sailing instructions. Often I would want to see the problem graphically, and at the words 'Take over' the navigator would slip into the steering position without any further word. Then the skipper could dive below to look at the chart, to make some special calculation of his own, to have a drink, put on a jersey, or to take a few seconds of rest.

Rest from the intense concentration of steering is important if the yacht is always to be steered at her best, so at racing stations I made a point of relaxing flat on my back for at least a minute in every hour at the tiller. The tactician-navigator needed to be an experienced racing skipper himself, who could understand what was in the skipper's mind and, thinking with him on all tactical aspects, give answers in the most useful form. Peter had these qualifications to a high degree; as a submarine navigator he was used to similar problems, he had experience as a Dragon-racing helmsman, and had ocean-raced in many oceans, including a long windward race some years before with me.

In charge forward at racing stations was the mate, George Wheatley, who similarly needed to be able to assess the skipper's thoughts so that he could be ready to carry out any order when it came. Our plan at racing stations was that any order affecting the sails or the trim went through the mate, to whom those on deck looked for their instructions. The degree of discretion left to the mate must always be a matter that is gradually evolved between him and his skipper by practice together; by our plan all sail changes and reefing were for the skipper to decide, while all trimming of sails when set was the responsibility of the mate; either could suggest within the realms of the other, but the responsibility was definite. Thus the skipper might comment: 'I reckon she needs a boom guy,' 'The spinnaker seems shy with the pole topped up so far'; while equally the mate could comment: 'It's getting a bit fresh for the ghoster,' or 'I reckon she'd just carry the spinnaker.'

In training races, or practices, there may be times when the skipper wants to direct sail-handling himself, and in this case he would probably hand over the tiller to the navigator and take over the mate's functions while explaining or demonstrating his needs.

Under the direction of the mate at racing stations came the other three men of our crew. Right forward as fore-deck man was usually Mike Tanner, who would hank on and remove headsails as they were shifted, rig and unrig the spinnaker poles, handle the anchor, and anything else that went on forward. Often when manoeuvring at close quarters the fore-deck man would be lent from the mate's department to the navigational side and act as forward look-out, reporting movements obscured behind the genoa direct to the cockpit.

The mate's other two men were normally stationed one at

the fore-end of the cockpit, ready to adjust the sheets, and the other lying on deck amidships, ready to move forward or aft as the mate directed. *Belmore*'s cockpit was not large, and I soon found that any more than one man stationed in it for sail-trimming would distract the helmsman and almost certainly foul his view of the compass and the sea ahead. When tacking, a second man was usually necessary in the cockpit to winch in the genoa sheets, but the moment that was done he would move back to his prone position on deck. *Belmore* was sensitive to fore-and-aft trim, and normally an extra man aft would add to the drag of her transon through the water.

We had won these two races handsomely in our class, so the crew of *Belmore* had formally taken their positions under my orders: George Wheatley, mate; Mike Tanner, second mate; Peter Paffard, navigator; Tim Sex and Roy Mullender, hands.

Each signed a formal agreement that he would sail under the orders of the skipper selected by the Royal Naval Sailing Association until released on return to Portsmouth in mid-August; each agreed to contribute to the costs of the yacht the equivalent of his normal pay for one week, and to pay his full messing costs, besides providing himself with all personal sailing equipment and uniform needed. He confirmed that he was sailing as a volunteer member of the crew, and would not hold the R.N.S.A. responsible for any accident or illness caused by the venture.

In return, all had been presented with the knitted woollen caps, coloured blue, white, and red, that were to be worn on formal occasions sailing in the yacht. Any further return he might get for his side of the bargain must come from satisfaction in whatever the crew could achieve on behalf of their Club, their Service, and their Country.

The two races, and several other outings under sail in the winter and early spring, had for me been the best part of the preparations. Working as part of the committee which organized the venture, I had for months slogged through mountains of administration; steady progress had tripped over grievous disappointments; apparently impassable obstructions had been by-passed by obstinate determination and whole nights of labour. This effort had fallen on many, but I was the fortunate one who had been selected to lead the venture.

Ready for sea

Now we were on our way; the crew was selected; the yacht was prepared and equipped; the plans were made. Even our preliminary training was completed, and we were outward bound.

Clear of the harbour, watch-racing routine was ordered, with special attention to the organization below decks. When racing, one of the biggest diversions from a quick reaction to changes in wind or weather can be the presence of food or its equipment in the cockpit. Never have I met a man who could steer really well while he also ate or drank, and never have I seen a watch on deck tend the sheets faithfully, tack, gybe, or reef readily, when there were plates on the winch handles, mugs among the sheets, and sandwiches in the hands. Concentrating upon sailing the yacht while on watch needed to be taught as a habit, especially among those who had cruised round an ocean-racing course, using the cockpit as pantry-cum-dining-room, with part-time employment in a bit of sailing in between. Green grass is good for picnics, but the tennis player who squatted round the net for snacks while he was playing with one hand would probably not be invited to the Centre Court again.

In an ocean racer, bent on winning against those with similar intentions, there must be a time for sailing and a time for eating; a man cannot serve his stomach and the sails at the same time. If the night watches are long and cold it would be better if each man of the watch on deck were relieved from his responsibilities for a few minutes to drink a cup of hot soup below, than that the deck be manned by a watch of semi-sailors, one hand to the cup and one to the ship. It is the instruments of eating, left skulking in the dark, that cause a man to slip-up on deck; they cause the compass to have a surprise deviation; they jam the runners, part the sheets, and generally make sailing more difficult than it need be.

Below decks the yacht should be designed for eating in comfort, drinking with satisfaction, and washing-up with efficiency. The limitation to living below is usually seasickness, and few are the crew that are not affected until they face it firmly. To win a Bermuda race the crew should learn to eat entirely below, and those who pine for the open spaces should be given a seasick pill and a firm answer; they can have ample of the open air during their own watch on deck.

Another habit that needs hard effort to eradicate is also a child of seasickness; this is the preference for discussion to

2   March sail drill in the Solent. George Wheatley (left), Peter Paffard (at the tiller), Roy Mullender, and Tim Sex

3   George Wheatley, mate   4   Mike Tanner, second mate

5 Tim Sex, third mate

6 Sail repairs on board M.V. *Ebro*. Mike Tanner and George Wheatley

action, which is a natural symptom of the illness. Seasickness leaves the mind clear but reduces physical energy, so that very clarity of mind flies to the rescue of the enervated muscles with such a delaying statement as 'We didn't do it that way in the *Dabchick*'. A suitable rejoinder in the early stages of training is merely 'Did the *Dabchick* win?'. But gradually the habit needs to be inculcated that discussion and reminiscence are excellent when below decks off watch, but the function of those on deck is to act; if those charged with making decisions are indecisive the yacht will be fortunate if she even finishes the race.

To spend a watch without eating or reminiscing may sound too high a price for winning, and perhaps the whole business of striving so hard to win a race may seem almost un-English to many good yachtsmen. I was spared the need to ponder over such ethics as my club had given me very definite instructions. They could not be achieved without such striving.

After a brisk night at sea the wind turned easterly as we came off Dover, setting up a chop with the tide in our favour. Past North Foreland, into the Thames Estuary, and the breeze died with the day, so at dusk there was little more than the floodtide to waft us through a maze of light-buoys and a procession of ships. When the tide checked its flow we let go the anchor near the entrance of the Medway River and slept until the dawn.

Next morning we sailed up to Chatham to meet the Nore branch members of our Association, and to give them a chance to see the yacht in whose venture they were shareholders; again we had an escort, this time one yacht which had sailed to greet us. Next day, when we sailed, the club fired a salute from their starting-gun, as though to send us off to a good start.

The River Thames, at least above Tilbury, is not greatly used by those yachtsmen who would cruise in peace and comfort of mind. But we had a job to do, so were bound to sail

B

up the river, accepting the fact that for a craft of the size of *Belmore*, dependent entirely upon sail, it was a more hazardous piece of water than mid-Atlantic. The Thames is a busy thoroughfare in which great liners, coasters, tugs, and strings of lighters are all busy, and each intent on making the fullest use of the tide; so that tide is itself a hazard to a sailing craft as well as a help. We in *Belmore* had a set time to reach the entrance of the Royal Docks in Gallions Reach by high water, so it was a race with a hundred obstacles. Our newly fitted echosounder, called the Hecta, proved of unexpected value in these waters, as when the river was so congested with passing and crossing traffic that the safety of *Belmore* seemed in hazard we could stand into water where the instrument showed that we had enough water to remain afloat, yet no corner-cutting coaster could join us due to her deeper draught.

During this river voyage Peter Paffard had a very full job as navigator and tactician. He had to forecast moves several tacks ahead, taking into account the bends in the river, any gaps in the traffic, the varying strength of the tide, and also the great factory buildings that deflected or shielded the wind. One factor soon became clear: however much the river turned on its course up to London Docks the wind would always be ahead in each leg; and wherever the floodtide ran fastest it would be certain that every other small craft would concentrate.

So long as the yacht was under way we managed to avoid all hazards, but soon after we secured alongside the dock entrance, waiting for permission to sail in, a tug swung her stern into *Belmore*; it was only a mere touch compared with the normal bouncing and shoving of lighters in the Thames, but to a small yacht with enamel topsides it was a heavy collision from which we were lucky to escape with no worse than a scraped side. 'You're not the only one,' sympathized a waterman. 'A ruddy lighter's just scraped down the side of *Britannia* in the Pool. Mucked up her enamel proper, it has.' The damage would need to be repaired before the Royal Yacht set forth on a princess's honeymoon next day, while at least we had ample time on our voyage to touch up *Belmore*.

The river voyage, the passage through the docks, and every part of the venture when the yacht was beyond her natural element of the open sea was an anxiety to me. The opportunities were numerous for some little incident that would disable the yacht, and bring to nothing the whole effort of so many people in preparing for the venture. It would be no consolation to me if the fault lay upon someone else; my orders and responsibilities were clear enough—'You are hereby directed to take the *Belmore* under your command'—and it was my responsibility that no act of man, no chance of weather, and no combination of circumstances should prevent me from starting the Bermuda race. Even the decision to sail the yacht round to the docks in London, and alongside the ship that was to carry her, came from previous experience of a near failure; ten years before, another yacht was put in my charge for a similar venture, and was moved to London by road in the usual manner for cargo going overseas; then came a strike with the ship almost fully loaded and ready to sail, while the yacht was still outside the docks. It was an exasperating time, but I would never forget the little Cockney docker, who listened to my appeal for a free passage through the pickets with his not too sympathetic fellows of a strike meeting, then stood up to start a mock book, offering to lay long odds that the little yacht loaded on a trailer nearby would either win the race across the Atlantic or sink on the way. His humour won the freedom of the dock gates, from which all guards, official or otherwise, were conveniently 'absent' at the right moment. This time the plan relied more upon water than the land; the yacht sailed under her own crew alongside the freighter in the docks, then her crew of naval men on leave were 'signed on' as hands in the freighter, and could be used at her Master's discretion to help hoist their yacht onboard. Soon after we arrived with the yacht alongside the Royal Mail Line freighter *Ebro*, Commander E. Bruce, R.N., Captain G. M. Wheatley, R.M., Lieutenant T. J. F. Sex, R.N., Lieutenant P. M. S. Paffard, R.N., Lieutenant M. G. C. Tanner, R.N., and P. O. El(A) J. R. Mullender became Supernumary Deckhands Bruce, Wheatley, Sex, Paffard, Tanner, and Mullender.

The simple solution to these problems would be to sail the yacht out to America, which is an easy voyage after reaching the Trade Winds, and would also give valuable sea practice to the crew. However, the time factor prevented this, as the long voyage under sail might take over six weeks to America. Our plan, and that of *Danegeld*, was to ship to Bermuda, taking stores and provisions to be left there until the start of the Transatlantic race, then sail north to America, arriving about four weeks after we had set out for London from Portsmouth. With this plan we used up every day of our three months' leave of absence from the Navy, while the owner of *Danegeld*, R. T. Lowein, Esq., was away from his dental practice in the Isle of Wight an even shorter time by sending *Danegeld* overland to London and himself flying home from Sweden.

It was a generous gesture of the Royal Mail Line that enabled our plan to be put into effect; out of friendship for the Royal Navy, and as a sporting contribution towards British participation in the important sailing areas, the Line agreed to ship our crew as supernumary hands, and made no charge for the yacht carried on deck. Bobbie Lowein, as an ex-naval man, was given the same facility for himself, while accompanying *Danegeld* embarked as normal cargo. We were lucky to have him with us; selected 'Yachtsman of the Year', for his achievement with *Danegeld* in 1959, he was an outstanding skipper besides an exceptionally well-informed sailing man. It was accepted that all of us would sleep onboard our yachts, and take meals with the ship's officers and twelve passengers in the saloon; but in practice we were lent some of the comfortable accommodation of the officers and crew; thus Bobbie Lowein and George shared the cabin reserved for a doctor, should one need to be carried; two others used the sick-bay bunks which would be vacant so long as the health of the crew was so good; two more shared the cabin aft provided for cattlemen when the cargo included livestock, while I had the pilot's cabin under the bridge.

The *Ebro* proved a particularly friendly ship. The yachtsmen had breakfast and lunch early to enable them to get more hours of work on their yachts; then, hungry from their hard efforts, they dined late with the passengers and senior officers of the ship. Inevitably in a ship at sea the Master is the guiding influence, whose every word and action comes in caricature from his pedestal as captain. We were fortunate indeed with Captain James Phillips; he was genial host to every one of his passengers, friend and guide to each one of his officers and crew, while the yachtsmen got the benefit of both. James Phillips was no slave to convention, and some of his pranks must have caused as much surprise to conventionalists, as they caused delight to the young in heart; he was the joy of his crew, and acting on their behalf he must sometimes have been a trial to his authorities ashore.

Our eleven-day voyage to Bermuda passed quickly. Six men, working perhaps through eight hours a day on behalf of an eleven-ton yacht, means that a great deal is done that few yachts can enjoy in normal sailing. She can be stripped down inside for careful painting of the difficult places; each item of her equipment can be sorted, tested, and replaced; each spare shackle and tube of grease can be stowed with unhurried care; and finally the long hard job of rubbing down the bottom can be done again and again, until the underwater surface can glide through the water without turbulence, and the muscles of arms and backs are tuned by this work to the needs of sailing the yacht.

Such fast progress on the yacht would be impracticable ashore in England, where life for all but hermits is tied to the complex pattern of social groups, to the telephone, the letter post, and to the convention of the shore; then an unhindered eight hours of concentration on one subject in a day can scarcely be achieved without offence to fellow creatures.

We also kept in practice with our navigation, working from the yachts stowed on the hatch-top immediately before the bridge.

'I don't know where you are,' hailed the Captain from the bridge one evening, as he saw me aiming my sextant at the evening stars, 'but my part of the ship expects to make Bermuda at dawn tomorrow.'

2

Practice in Bermuda

THE crew of *Belmore* was on deck early to watch the passage
of the *Ebro* through the reefs of Bermuda, and alongside the
wharf at Hamilton. The ship secured before breakfast-time,
but even at this early hour many sailing friends came on board
to offer welcome help.

I remembered just such an arrival eight years before, when
my impatience to get little *Samuel Pepys* sailing by noon after
her long voyage out in another Royal Mail freighter over-
whelmed even courtesy to those who greeted us. This time I
was determined to be more patient. I cast aside all idea of her
being afloat before lunchtime, added on six hours to make
certain of ample time, and then told the Commodore of the
Royal Bermuda Yacht Club that *Belmore* would arrive under
sail to make her call at 6 p.m. The club was less than half a
mile from the freighter, and Jerry Trimmingham offered to
have her towed; but I was anxious to be sailing the day we
arrived, so that the crew training could quickly get into its
stride.

Patience held out while the ship's derrick was rigged with
great care throughout the morning. The wind was fresh, and
the sea alongside too much for the original plan of stepping
the masts with the help of the freighter's derricks, so during
the dinner-break for the crew of *Ebro* we manhandled the two
masts over the side and carried them along the wharf to a
sheltered spot under the lee of the freighter's stern, where the

23

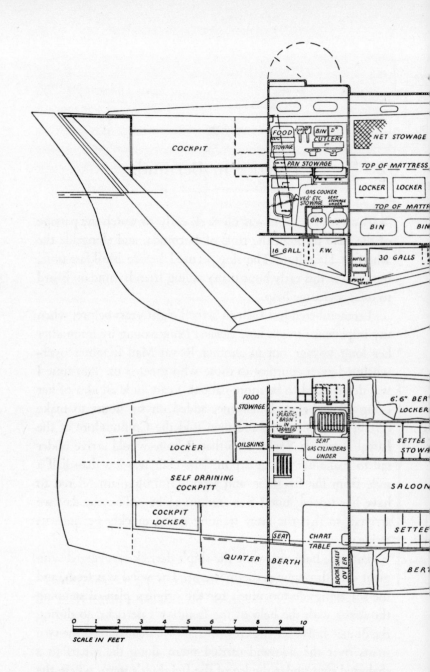

COCKPIT

FOOD ETC STOWAGE

CUP

BIN D° CUTLERY

NET STOWAGE

PAN STOWAGE

TOP OF MATTRESS

LOCKER LOCKER

GAS COOKER VEG° ETC STOWAGE

SEAT STOWAGE UNDER

TOP OF MATTR

GAS CYLINDERS

BIN BIN

16 GALL F.W.

BOTTLE STORAGE

30 GALLS

PUMP STRUM

FOOD STOWAGE

LOCKER

OILSKINS

PLASTIC BASIN IN DRAWER

SEAT GAS CYLINDERS UNDER

6' 6" BER LOCKER

SETTEE STOWA

SELF DRAINING COCKPITT

SALOON

COCKPIT LOCKER

SETTEE

QUATER BERTH

SEAT

CHART TABLE

BOOK SHELF OVER

BERT

0 1 2 3 4 5 6 7 8 9 10

SCALE IN FEET

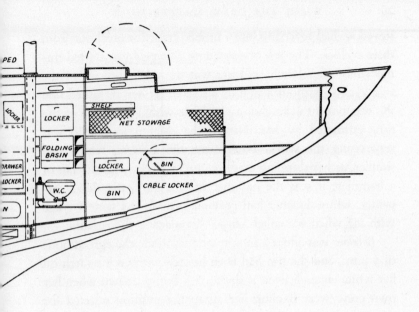

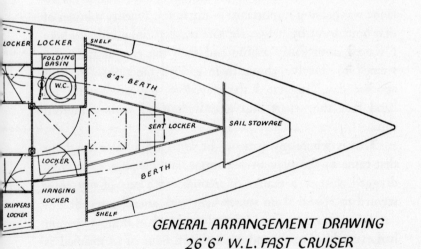

GENERAL ARRANGEMENT DRAWING
26'6" W.L. FAST CRUISER

L.O.A   36 FT 4 INS
L.W.L.   26 FT 6 INS
BEAM.   9 FT 6 INS
DRAFT.   6 FT 0 INS
DISPLACEMENT. 8·4 TONS.

THAMES MEASUREMENT
11 TONS

DESIGN BY: ILLINGWORTH & PRIMROSE. EMSWORTH. HANTS.ENGLAND

stevedore had agreed to hire a mobile crane for one hour from three o'clock. The job of unloading *Danegeld* was started immediately after lunch, and she was the more difficult of the two yachts; without a sign of a scratch on her varnished side she was put into the choppy harbour within a minute of the time estimated by Mr. Nixon, the chief officer, who was supervising the work. Next came the *Belmore*, which was simpler, as her shipping cradle came to pieces with the tap of a hammer; it was the hammer of Mr. Flux, the ship's carpenter, whose brother had previously made the same voyage with me when we sailed *Samuel Pepys* across the Atlantic.

Belmore was afloat a minute or two inside the agreed hour of 3 p.m., and she too had been hoisted without a scratch on her white enamel, even if she took a bump or two when her own crew were hauling her aft to the position selected for stepping the mast. We still had ample time in hand for the yacht club rendezvous, but the stevedore's time-limit on his crane was gaining importance in my mind. Twenty minutes of that hour went by before *Belmore* reached the position where I waited impatiently ashore and then the rest of the crew seemed to dissolve about their various functions. 'Perhaps another day,' suggested the stevedore, indicating with his hand that the wharf was already blocked with numerous cars.

That is where my patience broke; I let fly at everything that came in the way of our immediate purpose. Cars were dragged clear in a matter of seconds; each one of my crew seemed to appear from somewhere with amazing speed.

'*Danegeld*'s mast first,' I fiercely ordered, as Bobbie Lowein had everything ready and we had not. Four of us steadied as the mobile crane lifted; the mast swung into position, with Bobbie to guide its foot on to the sixpence he had put there for good luck. In a few more seconds he had directed us which rigging to set up, and the crane was lowering its jib again. Time

was running out, and the yachts had to be moved around for
Belmore to get within reach.

'Let's stop and put a kettle on for some tea,' one of my
crew suggested. My temper glowed white-hot at the idea of
such servitude to a handful of dried leaves. In an aura of sparks
the mast went up at the rush, and in under a minute runners,
shrouds, and forestays took the weight. Peter was up the mast
almost in the same breath to unhook the jib of the crane.

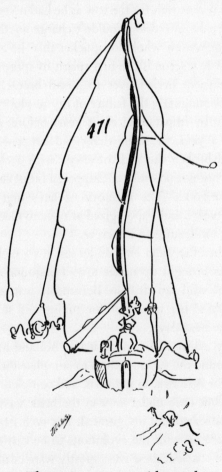

The mast went up with a rush

Then would have been a sensible time to pause, but once roused to such indignation I would allow no deviation from the objective of getting under sail as soon as possible, and took charge of the job myself. While Mike fitted the boom and rove the mainsheet, George looked enquiringly at the curves of the mast aloft, with the rigging set up as it came. 'Tuning's not on today's programme,' I snapped, 'but sailing is.'

'I'll see you at the yacht club,' said Bobbie as we hoisted the sails. He was to wait for the tow as he had no crew to help. 'By the way, the stevedore wouldn't charge anything for the crane. Things went a whole lot quicker than he expected.'

Within a few seconds the first splash of spray spotted the deck as the yacht heeled over to a stiff breeze. The spray brought back stingingly the failure of my resolution not to be carried away by impatience; eight years before, almost to a day and to a yard, the same thing had happened; then Ian Quarrie had broken the spell of anger with a cheerful 'I'm glad you've not got on oilskins, Skipper; a bit of cooling spray will do you good.' The memory of Ian's hint had lasted through the years, and I apologized at once to George for my overbearing intolerance to the crew.

We reached the yacht club under sail at six o'clock, just as *Danegeld* was brought up under tow. I announced that after the first successful sail drill in Bermudan waters the yacht would remain at her moorings for tuning and stowing until 3.30 p.m. the next day.

Next day ashore in Bermuda it was hot and humid while struggling round the various offices to complete the formalities of clearing for America, to get visas, and complete other shipping needs; but once under way in the brisk westerly breeze we all felt refreshed and invigorated. For each day a training plan was made up with the evolutions to be carried out, and the aim to be reached; these were mostly watch drills, done by a different watch in turn with the others observing.

Our normal watch-racing organization allowed for two men on deck, with either the skipper or the cook coming up for any evolution such as tacking, reefing, or sail-shifting. Thus each combination of three that might make up a watch, in turn tacked the yacht, and the time was taken from the sails drawing on one tack, until they were again drawing close-hauled on the other. Whichever team recorded the slowest time had the chance to better this until their time reached the standard.

Then came the same competitions with each stage of sail-shifting; the time was taken from the order 'shift' until the new sail was fully hoisted and drawing; forty-eight seconds was the best achievement for a shift from the large C.C.A. to the R.O.R.C. genoa; thirty-eight seconds was the record for the next shift down to a working jib. Two rolls in the mainsail came down to thirty-two seconds, and setting the full main from two rolls got to thirty-eight; setting trysail from full main was completed in one minute thirty-nine seconds.

Next came watch competition for emergency drills. For these the starting position was the watch of two men on deck with the skipper on his bunk. For a sudden hard squall likely to blow out the largest genoa, the time would be taken from the cry by the mate of the watch: 'Squall—emergency down genoa!' As soon as the helmsman saw the skipper beginning to emerge from the hatch he would jump forward to gather in the sail as the other man of the watch began to lower; for this drill the best time of each watch was nineteen seconds until the sail was mastered on deck.

Similar drill was practised for emergency lowering of the mainsail, which might be needed in various circumstances; for this evolution, starting with the same situation of two men on deck, the best watch time was forty-one seconds, but this was always at some risk of stoving in the head of the skipper in the cockpit, as the yacht had no topping lift to her main boom.

We also practised frequently various 'all hands' emergency drills; man overboard, fire, and rigging failure. For this last evolution a canvas bucket was kept ready with gear in it for immediate repair jobs. In every case the foreword 'emergency' to an order meant that those required from below should come on deck dressed as they happened to be, and without donning safety-belts. Perhaps one of the main purposes of the emergency drills was to show each man, and all might be immediately in charge of the vessel as helmsman, perhaps with the mate-of-the-watch overboard or in some difficulty, that he had only to use the word 'emergency' to get a strong party of men on deck within a few seconds. Such a word may be checked by reluctance to declare an emergency, unless its use is rehearsed freely.

After three days in Bermuda the times entered in the evolution log were certainly fast; but this was always in perfect conditions within the Bermuda coral reefs, with the crew in light clothing without oilskins. Wearing oilskins and safety-belts increased the times, and a sail-shift that takes half a minute in easy conditions might well take five times as long in rough weather and darkness.

One heading in the evolution log had only a blank. It was my plan that each man should compete in speed with a scramble aloft up the mast, and return to the deck down the runner backstays. One of my sons could easily do this in under a minute, although at the age of near fifty I took much longer, even after regular exercise aloft when the yacht lay close to my house before we left England. On starting to exercise this in Bermuda the first volunteer had such a struggle to reach even the lower cross-trees that there was little enthusiasm from anyone else; so I gave up that particular drill for some other occasion, feeling that their hands were still not hard enough to climb small-diameter wire rigging. In time Roy Mullender mastered this ability by persistent practice on his own, and probably this is the best way for a man to acquire the facility of running up the rigging; certainly those who claim that they can always go up if they have to, but will show it only in an emergency, are bluffing themselves. At sea the bosun's chair is not an easy answer for a job aloft; if the yacht is moving jerkily a ride aloft in the bosun's chair can be really hazardous for someone unused to working up the mast.

The conditions we met in Bermuda were perfect for elementary crew drills, but the results were over-flattering for those preparing to ocean race. A lesson that can be learnt in sheltered waters in two days may well need twenty days of open-sea time to reach the same standard for rough-weather night work. Perhaps the pace was forced too much in this basic instruction; once a really good time had been returned by such an evolution as shifting to trysail from mainsail I assumed that the drill was known; in practice the steps of the dance need to be more firmly implanted as habits if all is to go well for the same drill on a dark rough night. The element of fear snatches away most skills that have not become second nature.

On the fourth day in Bermuda, with a few hours of sail drill each afternoon, I felt we were ready to set off for more advanced practice, so we finished our sail for the day in the quiet little harbour of St. George's; from there it was only a mile to the open ocean through the Town Cut, which always gave an interesting beat one way, as the wind funnelled up and down its narrow gorge.

It had been planned that next morning His Excellency the Governor would come out with us for two hours of sail drill; then later in the evening we would set off from the island, paced by other ocean-racing yachts for the first night. The *Belmore* lay alongside the wharf of the hospitable St. George's dinghy club, and by 9 o'clock next morning her looks were a pride to us all; when a fly landed on the enamel topside,

George was on the spot in a second to wipe off the footmarks with his chamois leather! A police officer arrived with a message that His Excellency was unwell, so I rang up Government House to find that Lady Gascoigne was prepared to represent her husband at sea in the small ocean-racer. We were delighted that she could come, and we enjoyed demonstrating the slick sail drill that had been learnt largely in the last four days; but the wind was so light that the storm sails looked rather ridiculous, and the spinnaker was pathetic as it drooped half-filled.

Back ashore I spent some time on the telephone without success, trying to achieve a marine weather forecast. It was easy enough to get a recorded message that told me the temperature on the bathing-beaches, and perhaps even the appropriate model of bikini suited to the day. I persisted that this was not the information needed for a yacht bound on an ocean passage, and was then informed by the same airport authority that the weather was confidential and could not be disclosed except to an authorized person. Secrecy over affairs controlled by the Almighty enraged me, so I demanded to speak with whoever was the highest authority at the airport. 'He may not be very sympathetic,' I was warned. 'You see, we told him that the sea would be calm for fishing, but his boat was knocked about by rough seas and he's just returned rather angry.' This explained the weather secrecy from the airport, so I turned for help from an American naval commander who happened to be passing the dinghy club.

He listened to my tale of airport secrecy with sympathy. 'That's crazy,' he said with indignation. 'How can the weather be secret!' He pointed out the ship which he commanded and advised me to go onboard to get the information I needed.

'And just what report do you want?' he asked.

'All I want to know is where I can find a real gale to practise in.'

7   The skipper walks aloft

8 The British sloop *Danegeld*, twelfth overall in the Bermuda race fleet; she raced on across the Atlantic to Sweden in twenty-five days

The destroyer captain looked down at *Belmore*; then he looked enquiringly into my eyes. 'You know,' he said with sympathy, 'it's you that's crazy. Of course the weather should be secret.'

Whether we were crazy or not, his ship gave us every assistance with traditional naval efficiency. A radio signal was sent off to Washington and shortly afterwards a special report came back. It told of a chain of depressions moving eastwards across the Western Atlantic with their centres passing some 300 miles north of Bermuda. 'There is a gale warning in force now,' the navigating officer told me, 'but you can't catch up that particular one. What speed can you make?'

I explained that sailing-boats were not too accurate as speed-makers, but if the wind was reasonably friendly we might make good five knots. He twirled his dividers and read off the latitude scale. 'Then I suggest you steer due north for three-fifty miles, and wait until a gale makes the rendezvous. I reckon it'll be about Tuesday when we pick up your Mayday signals; cursed if we are not duty destroyer that day.'

'Don't worry,' I answered. 'We've only an emergency transmitter, and it can't be picked up more than fifty miles away, so it will be a week before any ship happens to come close enough to hear.'

'That would still be us,' he retorted. 'We return to Norfolk next week.'

C

3

Search for a Gale

Armed with a sheaf of naval signals giving the life history and prospects of almost any gale in the northern hemisphere between San Francisco and the Azores, I returned to the yacht and we sailed off from St. George's Harbour. Before the gale rendezvous *Belmore* had another closer one with the yachts *Danegeld* and *Doncherry*; Bobbie Lowein had raised his crew from Bermuda yachtsmen, as his own crew had still to reach Bermuda, while *Doncherry* had on board most of the crew that was to race her against us in the Bermuda race under her owner, Sir Bayard Dill.

All three of us had agreed to race northwards through the night, and then the other two would turn back at some time to practise the approach to Bermuda that would be needed for the actual race. Neither of these two yachts would be ready to leave for America until some days later than *Belmore*, so it might have been better to wait in Bermuda and then sail a practice race the whole way up to America, but I was anxious to get gale practice while gales were still frequent in those waters, knowing that each week as the summer came on reduced the chance of bad weather.

In light conditions the three yachts paced each other, with a short spinnaker run, a light reach over a lop of sea from ahead, and then a light-wind beat; in *Belmore* we felt well satisfied with her performance under each condition. As each helmsman finished his trick I sailed back astern of the next

34

yacht so that the new helmsman would be set the task of overtaking.

Next morning we were on our own with the yacht in her watch-racing organization. For this two mates of watches, George and Mike, split the time, using standing four-hour watches; thus each mate had the same watches every day so that he could grow accustomed to the routine. The other three men provided the second hand of the watch, and also one acted as cook for twenty-four hours at a time; the second hands split the dog watches, so that the individuals of any watch of two men would frequently change, and all become familiar with working together as a pair. As skipper I took no watch, but was always immediately ready for the deck through the night, and always available to decide upon any sail changes at any time.

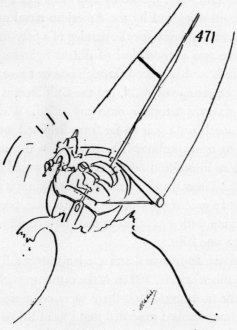

'Seasickness was no better'

After twenty-four hours of light conditions the wind increased and soon a steep sea brought heavy motion to the yacht and a bout of seasickness. Inwardly I rejoiced at this in the hope that the worst seasickness would be over before our gale rendezvous. Yet another twenty-four hours of this motion, with a good many practice sail-shifts, took a great deal out of the crew; two more rolls in the mainsail, to make a total of five, took a laborious three minutes instead of the calm-weather practice time of thirty-two seconds; seasickness was no better, and exhaustion increasing, so I ordered watch-cruising for eight hours from noon; this required only one man on watch, with no need to shift sails to each wind change, and enabled everyone to make up his lost sleep. At 8 p.m., around dusk, we went back to watch-racing with our gale rendezvous less than fifty miles ahead.

It was on 24th May, at 0300 by ship's time, that we reached the rendezvous suggested by the American naval officer, and we held on at seven knots for the first leg of a fifty-mile-square search. There was a good deal of distant lightning, and the radio crackled; we had passed through one or two rain squalls without much change of wind, but the Gulf Stream feeling of uneasiness clamped strongly onto my mind. Was it really sensible to search for a gale so far from help and with a crew so unused to ocean sailing? The coward in me said it was absurd, and an imposition on the crew who would have gales enough in the Transatlantic race. But what logic was left to me, in the path of a gale at 3 o'clock in the morning, persisted that only by playing with a gale in our own time could we hope to race through one later.

As the dawn approached and the barometer fall remained slow, I felt more at ease. When Mike came up with Peter to take over the morning watch there were no more squalls in sight, and things looked so settled that I went below and took off my oilskins; the barometer was falling faster, but I had every hope of stars still being unobscured by cloud when the horizon would be right for sights in about another hour. The motion was less than the previous night, with waves around six feet high and fairly regular, so I reckoned on accurate observations.

Suddenly the regular roll ceased as though she had run into calm water. 'There's a squall,' said Mike down the hatch. Fastened to the chart-table with a belt, I had not at once noticed that she was heeled well over.

I donned oilskins quickly, annoyed with myself for having taken them off. The first glance showed that Mike, very much on his toes, was ready to dart forward the moment I appeared. Only then did I appreciate the drastic change in the weather. Rain was driving horizontally in great dollops, driven by wind of real power. But the night seemed oddly quieter; the deluge had flattened out the waves as though a bucket of cold water had drenched over a simmering saucepan. There was a low whistle in the rigging, but the wind was so steady that this lost much of its effect, and the main noise came from the swish of the bows creaming through the flat sea as the eleven-ton yacht planed like a Firefly dinghy.

The wind was abaft the beam, and for a second or two I hesitated, thinking that this gale-driven rush in the darkness was too great a thrill to miss.

But already there was a slight change in the tune of the rigging whine. It was beginning to squeal and we would be lucky to get the genoa down intact if it was left much longer.

'Down genny' had scarcely formed on my lips when Mike began to lower. The moment the halyards were started that sail became like a creature gone mad; hooked to the rigging in their safety harness, Mike and Peter had a tough time to master the stampeding rage of terylene. But her speed seemed no less without it, as the yacht hurled through the water; she was unbalanced under mainsail only.

'Stand by trysail, sir?' Mike asked. I felt this was only a squall, and told him to take four rolls in the mainsail, after first throwing overboard the lightning-conductor which was ready attached to the rigging. Tim Sex, cook of the day, was already on deck in oilskins to back up the watch; the three of them huddled around the mast to roll down reluctant reefs.

It was just then that the yacht was struck by lightning.

For a fraction of time sparks flashed from the winch handle in Mike's hand; then came a crack like a six-inch gun heard from too near the muzzle, and all on deck were blinded. I could feel the hammering of the mainsail slides in the mast-track, and sensed that those forward must be shocked. They might have let go.

'Emergency all hands,' I shouted down the hatch. Those below had shot out of their bunks with the thunder-clap, but were dazed also.

In a second or two my eyes began to see again, and my ears recovered from the crack. I could her Mike's laugh as he chortled: 'I seem to have got that earth-wire over the side about in time.'

'All right, George,' I said, as the mate appeared in the hatch, almost naked. 'Emergency over. Watch below not needed.'

That was only the first of the lightning; many more flashes played around us not very far away. The wind was still increasing and it could not be long before the sea would build to the gale, however heavy the rain.

'Drop the mainsail all together, Mike,' I shouted. 'Boom on deck. The trysail afterwards.'

Perhaps I was wrong about the squall passing over quickly. There seemed more to it than that. 'Hold on to the trysail, I want to have a look at things in slow time.'

So the yacht sailed on under bare poles, driven quite fast by the weight of the wind on the hull, mast, and rigging.

Peter took the tiller, and I went below to look at the barometer; it had dropped a good deal since midnight, and the indications all suggested that this was the gale promised by the U.S. Navy. Not just a Gulf Stream squall.

On deck again we leisurely read the hand anemometer for the wind speed; with no sails to cause eddies the reading would be accurate. 'Forty-one knots,' I quoted, standing on the mast winches with the instrument some eleven feet above the mean sea level, 'and it's as steady as holding it out of the car window.'

That meant force nine on the Beaufort scale, which compares mean wind strength at a height of thirty-three feet. Usually in a gale the wind is constantly changing its strength as it gusts and eases; it is the turbulence which may carry away sails, and this most commonly comes with the rear of the depression or on the passage of a cold front. The steady hard wind we were experiencing as the barometer fell was far less dangerous, and splendid for first-stage gale practice.

We all had a good look at the conditions, as by then the dawn was breaking. It was a gale, a strong gale, but with no sail hoisted all could see that there was nothing to worry about; a good deal of noise by that time, and we had even been struck by lightning without any ill effect.

'Check the speed,' I ordered Peter.

'Five point one, sir,' he answered. 'All those sails only give her a couple more knots than she is making under bare poles.'

'Yes,' I answered, 'but they can make her go to windward, and now she is running; we'll try. Slow time, Mike, I'll have the trysail and heavy-weather jib first.'

In the next few hours the gale went through a textbook pattern. The thunder passed on; the rain stopped, and then came again; the wind eased and blew up once more with greater turbulence; the seas built higher and became confused as the wind changed its direction; the barometer checked its fall and climbed upwards faster than it went down. Through this changing sequence of the gale's life we shifted headsails and brought her gingerly round with the wind before the beam for short legs of broad-reaching, as we practised the normal gale routine for a small sailing craft in the open ocean. We never came hard on the wind, nor forced the pace in any way; the plan was to get used to the feel of a gale in a small yacht; to treat it as a normal event, with its need of a straightforward routine and good oilskins. There was no call for epics at that stage, and I regretted the emergency cry for all hands, even if this had been cancelled before the watch below reached the deck.

Each gale has a personality of its own, usually with marked variations from the normal; so it is hard enough to practise gale drill without any crisis at all. This one had done us exceptionally well; it had come just when and where we expected it; it had gone through almost the normal paces, and had only caught us on the wrong foot when the lightning struck her and temporarily blinded me.

This gale had one more trick to play, but the mate of the watch foresaw it as he sailed her through a regular sea whose waves averaged eleven feet from crest to trough. The wind was force six, so under real racing conditions we should already have set the reefed mainsail.

'Looks like the edge of a front ahead, sir,' reported Mike just ten hours after the gale had struck us. 'I'll clear away the mainsail ready.'

As the cloud-edge drove past to leave clear sky the wind fell suddenly to nil. One moment the yacht was making six and a half knots under trysail and working jib, then the next she was becalmed, rolling like a thing gone mad. The sea itself was taken unawares, and for a few minutes white horses reared up all round us, although there was not a breath of wind to drive them.

Soon the white horses realized that the hunt had gone elsewhere; they faded away to leave the ocean furrowed by a lumpy swell, over which a new breeze crept hesitatingly from the west.

'I see what you mean about the Gulf Stream, sir,' mentioned Mike Tanner, when he had set the full mainsail and big genoa. 'It is a bit different from the Channel.'

4

Electronic Aids

THE gale was over. It had reached force nine, which was as strong a wind as we were likely to meet during the whole summer, although the fast movement of the depression that formed it gave no time for high seas to build up. No damage had been done to equipment, and all of us had gained something. Perhaps it needs a gale, faced together, for a handful of sailing-men to become a real ocean-racing crew, whatever their individual ability.

Each member of my crew took on a new significance after that gale; it was like the stamp of 'tested' on every shackle in the rigging. There was George, short, wiry, and compact; his curly reddish hair, salt-sprayed by the gale, competing with his dapper military moustache to show which was the real George; but whether the sea dog or the dapper Royal Marine officer showed strongest, each was as tough as the other. It was probably George's exploits in the Malayan jungle that had taught him to sleep in almost impossible conditions when off duty, and perhaps a combination of deeds by land and sea that enabled him to 'switch off' any feelings that could sense discomfort. There was one point on which George and I could not agree, even after the gale; I had never before been called 'sir' by my mate when skippering an ocean racer, but he persisted; it was not so much military habit, he surprisingly argued later when half a bottle of whisky had been absorbed

42

in the discussion, it was more the pirate side of him that liked it that way.

Mike Tanner, too, showed new qualities in the gale, and his judgement proved as dependable as it had been in quieter conditions; he could not ignore discomfort as George did, but even sleeplessness did not detract from a cheerful acceptance of the worst conditions. The hammering of a gale at sea in a small yacht soon deadens most men, with the additional burden of oilskin clothing and the extra effort of fighting for balance with each step and movement; yet gales had an invigorating effect on Mike.

The same was so of Tim, in a different way. Tim was always an astute observer, ready to amuse with a swift repartee or ridicule some careless statement. With the gale, as with a person, Tim's mind let nothing pass him, and he reacted quickly to any change of the wind or weakening of the weather.

Peter had already sailed with me before in bad weather; tall, with long limbs and a quiet voice, he was more used to rough seas at close quarters than any of them, and was content with mild sarcasm at the expense of a violent wave that drenched him.

Roy was a large man for whom the crowded small yacht often restricted his movement; yet the gale allowed him more scope to use his limbs and his muscles to their full strength. He seemed actually to enjoy the gale, as he was deeply sensitive to the blending of personalities in the struggle for an immediate common purpose.

A gale is the ultimate purpose of so much that makes up the work as well as the equipment of an ocean-racing yacht; to learn habits for a distant objective can often feel restrictive and thwarting, but when the gale comes for which most of these habits were designed then there is satisfying simplicity in the pattern.

Yet even with the gale past and the crew proved, it was hard to feel at ease when sailing in the Gulf Stream area. Many are the yachts that have lost sails, blown to ribbons in a squall, on this same voyage through the Stream in May, and we could not afford new sails, except as an essential racing necessity. The Gulf Stream is a current of warm water which wanders through the ocean on an uncertain course, within fairly wide limits; it is warmer than the ocean water on which it floats, and is therefore quite readily deflected to a new track. Usually the Stream itself, in the area we were sailing, is about fifteen to twenty miles wide and floats on the ocean as a wide river a couple of hundred fathoms deep in the centre, although the sea bottom is a thousand fathoms beneath it. The general direction of the current is to the eastwards, eventually to split with one branch going north of the British Isles and one curving south along the Iberian Peninsula; but locally this stream may meander and even curl directly against the general direction, in the same way as a shallow river wanders through water meadows.

Within the current itself the water may be moving at five knots, and there is often a conspicuous swirl, like a tide-race, where its edge meets the ocean water. Even a moderate wind blowing against this fast-running stream will cause a protest of steep angry seas.

On the evening after the gale we were around the middle of the Gulf Stream area, and at 10 p.m. Roy reported that he felt we were in the Stream itself from the change of temperature. He was right, as the hourly count of radio pips broadcast from Nantucket Consolan Station showed we were being set to the east; by chance the wind was from the west, so there was no rough sea, but instead a distinctive motion that gave the yacht an uneasy rocking-horse movement. At 2.30 a.m. George saw a squall coming, and in a few seconds it struck with heavy rain and a strong wind from the west; there was lightning all round, but not too close, and the wind lacked the fierce insistence of the previous night's gale. 'Take four rolls in the main,' I ordered. 'Cook on deck, stand by the genoa halyards.' Peter hurried on deck in his oilskins, while the watch were busy with the mainsail.

Five minutes later the wind dropped from its thirty-knot squall to the fifteen knots we had felt before it came. But somehow when the full sail had been set again the boat now had quite a different feel to her. I was puzzled for a minute or two, feeling that perhaps the sails were not properly trimmed; it was Roy who first noticed that we had got off the rocking-horse. It was soon cooler and the radio dots confirmed that we were no longer being set to the east. But, most of all, that strange feeling of Gulf Stream tension had gone.

After a quiet day of calm seas and light northerly winds I was below fiddling with the Consolan radio when Peter came down from the cockpit, well before the end of his middle watch; he moved oddly down the vertical ladder under the main hatch.

'What's wrong?' I asked.

'Don't know,' he answered in obvious pain. 'My back hurts like blazes.'

Peter was the ship's doctor, so it was I who helped him into an upper bunk, and gave him a pain-killing pill. 'It should be all right after a rest,' Peter said hopefully; but I doubted this. A back pain severe enough to make Peter abandon his watch seemed to me a definite injury; a fit young man of twenty-four is unlikely to be disabled by rheumatics. However, we were only about a hundred miles from the coast of New England and I hoped we would soon be able to get the advice of a doctor.

Next morning his pain was worse. Peter himself had stowed the medicine-box, but I had checked through its contents. 'We've seen two U.S.S. warships and might meet another,' I told him, 'but before you could be transferred at sea you'd need a shot of morphia.'

'It's all there, Skipper,' Peter answered. 'What worries me is that I'm not doing my job.'

We had spoken by Morse to an American warship a few hours before this to ask how *Belmore* showed on her radar screen; she told us that the yacht showed up well, but as visibility decreased with the evening we rigged a special radar reflector as an extra precaution. During the evening we covered only a handful of miles each watch in the lightest of airs from the north, so lingered helplessly for some time in the shipping routes, blowing a foghorn which would probably be unheard against the engine noises of a ship.

With the dawn—it was the 27th May—the fog became really thick. I estimated we were some twenty-five miles from Montauk Point. The wind veered to south-east and with spinnaker set we ran northwards at a comfortable five knots. At breakfast-time I told Peter—who was not hungry—'With this wind we can be in New London in six hours; that is if only I can find the way through the fog.'

The problem was to find our way in, and at that moment the sea felt about as crowded with ships' fog sirens as there might seem to be buses to a cyclist at Hyde Park Corner. The first gateway to enter was the channel into Block Island Sound; it was thirteen miles from lighthouse to lighthouse, or radio beacon to radio beacon, but the actual deep-water channel in the middle was a good deal less. We had last seen the sun and horizon eighteen hours beforehand, so our landfall in the fog would depend on electronic aids if I were to get Peter to a doctor quickly. We had an excellent echo-sounding machine, radio help from the single Consolan station on Nantucket, and a whole regiment of radio beacons, but they tended to overlap their frequencies. Then there were also our ears, and eyes that could see no more than an uncertain hundred yards. All this should be enough, so long as careful attention was paid to all information that was available.

It was the navigator's big moment; yet it was on behalf of our navigator that all the hurry was needed; Peter, the navigator and 'doctor', lay on his bunk disabled. I took on the navigation, while George took charge of the watch on deck as we sailed towards an unseen lee shore at about five knots; a long swell had rolled in from the south-east since the dawn.

If a vessel could sail straight at a radio beacon, as a plane flies at one, electronic navigation would be quite simple; but there's no known way of sailing your yacht at a safe height above the radio beacon, nor even above the land it stands upon, nor yet above the shoals that surround it. So radio navigation afloat remains an art more than a precise science; in a small yacht at least, and with amateur operators, the bearings are never entirely accurate, nor always consistent.

The best method is to plot on the chart a continuous track of estimated positions allowing for the course and speed of the yacht, besides the tide she should experience; then each extra item of information, such as radio bearings, soundings, and Consolan, are also plotted on with their times. In practice they seldom agree exactly, but the navigator should be able to tell approximately where the yacht has got to, and, just as important, how accurate his estimate is likely to be. Safe navigation requires the assumption that the vessel is at her worst position relative to the nearest danger; this works all right until you need to pass between two dangers an equal distance on either side.

Audible signals, in this case the foghorns on Montauk Point and Block Island, can be a great help in a thick fog, except that when approaching with the wind astern, as *Belmore* was doing, fog horns are seldom heard until fairly close.

However, we were fortunate, and managed to hear the horn of Montauk when soundings and Consolan suggested we were still a couple of miles south of the coastline. Once that was heard, a stop-watch showed the time difference between the receipt of radio and audible signals transmitted simultaneously; from that came an accurate distance of the lighthouse, and with such synchronized checks every few minutes we were able to vector the yacht towards Phelps Ledge buoy, four miles east of the Montauk Point; this buoy marked the edge of the channel.

The tidal stream was with us so I plotted the rapid progress towards this buoy, while those on deck listened intently for the gong on the buoy.

'One cable to go. Right ahead,' I passed up the hatch.

'Half a cable——'

I was interrupted by a cry from the cockpit.

'There's a church bell; fairly close, starboard quarter.'

The directional radio aerial almost fell out of my hand, and I'll swear that the echo-sounder needle gave a jolt. The nearest land to starboard, by my reckoning, should be Block Island, six miles away.

'Could it be a gong ahead?' I asked.

'No, it's a bell, and nearly astern,' came the reply.

'Well, I think it's abeam,' said the look-out forward; 'and so close that we ought to see it.'

'It must be the buoy,' I told George. 'But we'll have to confirm it by sighting. Down spinnaker and turn towards it.'

The yacht was turned and tacked towards the sound, making slow progress against the tide.

'Perhaps in America they keep churches in the middle of the channel,' suggested Tim. 'Very handy for returning seamen. Wedding bells, I think.'

Not only did it sound like church bells to me, but the sound varied so much in direction that I could almost agree that there were a couple of them.

'A church and a chapel, perhaps,' put in Tim.

Suddenly Phelps Ledge buoy appeared through the fog less than a hundred yards ahead; another wisp of fog rolled down and it was lost to sight again.

'Set spinnaker,' I ordered, and gave the course for the Race, which is the eastern gateway to Long Island Sound, and the stream runs through it at upwards of five knots. There is no radio beacon on the Race Rock, and soon I got lost among the earphone sounds after several hours at the job.

'We should be close on to Cerberus Shoal, George,' I said, 'but the soundings show no change. Can you hear the whistle buoy?'

'No,' answered George, 'but I can hear several ships under way, so we ought to be all right.'

The confusion of radio sounds got worse in my mind, and I could not pick up the beacon on Little Gull Island, which should have been my best aid. The tidal stream was then in our favour, so we were moving fast towards the Race or the shoals that bounded it.

'Lower spinnaker,' I ordered. 'I'm not too certain about our position.'

'I'll have a go, sir,' suggested George. 'You've been stuck among the amps for too long.' George twiddled the tuning dials, then rotated the directional receiver in his hand for five minutes, while I went on deck in the fog for a change of view.

'She's quite all right,' he spoke up the hatch. 'Just about on the dead reckoning.'

We hoisted the spinnaker, and the Belmore sailed on at six knots over the ground, egged on by the tidal stream. Ten minutes later the fog lifted to the southwards to show Gardiner's Island five miles away; soon it became clear ahead, to show the Race Rock just where it should have been. The radio and echo-sounder had led us faithfully through the fog, and the only fault had been in my own mind, befuddled after several hours of intense work on the headphones.

D

We sailed on in sunshine, passing through the Race itself beside a nuclear submarine which rampaged past us on the surface giving the impression of power as from another world; then we turned in her flattened wake towards New London. It was a Friday afternoon and I wondered how long it would take to clear Customs and immigration authorities before Peter could get medical attention.

I need not have worried, as *Belmore* had scarcely entered the harbour when a U.S. naval motor-boat turned beside us, and two naval officers asked permission to come on board; one was British and the other American, but both were on the staff of the United States admiral commanding submarines in the Western Atlantic, and they came mutually to offer assistance to visiting British yachtsmen representing the Royal Navy. This help was what we wanted most of all, so, with a U.S. naval commander as pilot, we sailed on up the Thames River to berth the *Belmore* in the middle of a pack of submarines. A minute after the yacht was secured, Peter was in an ambulance on the way to hospital; and after a warm welcome from the base captain the rest of us were well looked after by people who understood sea passages in crowded conditions.

Through all our visits to many harbours, bays, and inlets in America, one of the most valuable aids proved the hospitality of a washing-machine. Three months in a yacht with each man limited to a small locker for his clothes presented a difficult problem in domestic organization, if the crew was always to be well turned out when in harbour or in sight of others.

For this first introduction to washing-machines in America we started a mock sail-shifting organization, with the halyard man to work the door, fore-deck man to shift clothes, and tactician to keep the times.

'That's all gone today,' explained a black U.S. able seaman. 'Jus' throw in the clothes and the soap powder; turn the

'Could we borrow the washing-machine, please?'

switch and go away. Dat machine will wash, rinse, and dry; just as you sets it on the dial.'

'Why on earth didn't we fit one to *Belmore*?' protested Tim. 'The machine could shift the genoa, trim the sheets, and bag the spinnaker; all with the setting of a dial. It would even take the time for you, Skipper.'

5

Long Island Sound

OUR arrival at New London on the evening of 27th May, with one man ill, meant that we missed by a narrow margin the storm trysail race. This was the last chance for a real overnight race before the Bermuda race started, and would have been most valuable in enabling *Belmore* to enter a real long-distance in good company, of a length to give genuine ocean-racing practice to the mates-of-the-watches. We could rehearse many aspects of such a race by crew drill, passages in racing routine, and short races, but only by actual ocean races could the mates-of-watches gain ocean-racing experience.

However, we enjoyed a weekend of rest and re-stowing at the submarine base, while waiting for a report on Peter's health. On the last day of May, a long weekend holiday being over, the doctor gave me an encouraging report on Peter, who he thought should be able to join us by the end of the week, quite fit for rigorous sailing. So we sailed off eastwards down Long Island Sound to join in as many races as possible, and meet the American yachtsmen against whom we were to compete in the two ocean races.

On the way down the Thames River *Belmore* called on the U.S. Coastguard Academy, some of whose yachts were entered for the Bermuda race as part of the training for Coast Guard midshipmen, under the lead of their officers and instructors. Largest for the race was the seventy-foot overall-length *Petrel*, which was to be skippered in the race by

Commander Noreau with a doctor, four lieutenants, and twelve others in the crew; but even this use of sail training was dwarfed by the barque *Eagle* of 1600 tons, which was about to set forth for Europe manned by future officers of the Academy.

Some of the Academy officers had seen over *Belmore*, and we had been on board their yachts, but Roy was still missing when we were ready to sail. At last he was sighted, up the foremast of the *Eagle*, where he perched on the topgallant yard with his sketching pad.

Clearing New London at dusk, we made a night passage along the centre of Long Island Sound, which averages some fifteen miles in width; for this passage sailing speed was unimportant, and each mate-of-the-watch was instructed to concentrate on navigation, in which the skipper would take no part except as cook; visibility was poor, and the exercise became more interesting for Mike Tanner when he discovered that a light-vessel shown on the chart with a radio beacon was in fact a buoy with no beacon, as the chart was not up to date; such are the practical trials of a yacht navigator. Winds were light, and the eighty-mile passage to City Island on the fringe of New York took nearly twenty-four hours; the navigation was good enough, in that we got there without running aground, but the skipper's cooking was considered successful only in that no one actually starved.

At City Island we secured alongside the famous Nevins yard, and I went to call in his neighbouring sail-yard office on a fellow member of the R.N.S.A., Ernest Ratsey. It was as though we had really got to the centre of our rivals, several of which were secured all around us, and in front of the Ratsey office was *Finisterre* herself, the yawl little bigger than *Belmore*, which all the world of ocean racing was out to beat after her double victory in the two past Bermuda races.

Also in the office, where Ernest Ratsey was busy getting sails from the testing bath so that we could use it to wash ourselves, was Colin Ratsey, whose *Golliwog* was another special rival, and had beaten *Belmore* by only fifty-six minutes, to be second to *Finisterre* in the last Bermuda race. Yet surrounded by such keen rivals we foreigners were given the warmest welcome and presented with anything that Ernest Ratsey felt would help our chances in the race. 'You know, Ernest,' I protested in our cockpit that evening, 'I believe you'd even give us Colin's mainsail if you thought it would make *Belmore* go faster.' 'Perhaps so,' Ernest Ratsey answered. 'But then we'd have to make *Golliwog* a new one overnight.'

Ernest Ratsey, his brother Colin, and son Colin, discussed on board *Belmore* every detail of her sails and their own sails and equipment. However intense the racing competition at sea, there was certainly no secrecy about equipment among ocean-racing rivals for the Bermuda race.

Next day we all visited New York; it was a yachting pilgrimage to the New York Yacht Club, of which I had been made honorary member for the visit, and I particularly wished all members of my crew to see this premier of American yachting clubs, with its famous model room; in this is a model of each challenger for the America's Cup beside her rival defender, and among them was the cup itself. With models of many other renowned craft, this room is the high altar of the sport of yachting, and I felt it would inspire us all with the long tradition of hard-contested races in American waters.

That evening I met John Lowein, an Englishman in New York, who was also to be our rival as navigator to his brother in *Danegeld*. John Lowein had already helped us by sending special charts from America, and again went out of his way to find me the best radio equipment for picking up American time-signals at sea. We were 3000 miles from home, but even her rival crews did everything possible to see *Belmore* was equipped to her best advantage to compete against them.

Next day we sailed from City Island in a stiff breeze. George was acting as skipper for the approach to Oyster Bay, and met all the wind he needed as he beat up to an anchorage off the Seawanhika Corinthian Yacht Club, where many more of our future rivals lay. I met Gabriel Giannini, from California, whose forty-nine-foot-overall-length yawl *Pacifica* was entered for a Transatlantic race to Spain after reaching Bermuda; later we both dined with Commodore and Mrs. Henry Du Pont, whose new sloop *Cyane* would be racing with us all the way to Sweden. During the evening there was mention of some navigational tables I had not seen; first thing next morning a copy of these was passed on board from a dinghy.

It was Saturday, 4th June, and we had been invited to enter that day and the next for a series of two twenty-five-mile races organized by the New York Yacht Club. For these races there was an entry of some fifty yachts, many of them large ones, and nearly all of the type we would be racing against to Bermuda. The waters of Long Island Sound are well known for the tricks they play on strangers, so I determined to pick on a likely rival, rating slightly higher than *Belmore*, and try to follow her movements. None could be better than *Finisterre*, and we were fortunate to make a good start a couple of lengths to leeward of her just as she crossed the line. To my joy we actually beat her to the first mark to windward, but on a long spinnaker run she got well ahead; however, the wind was light at the down-wind buoy, and as *Finisterre* was forced to round the mark alongside a larger yacht *Belmore* slipped inside to get ahead once more for a reach.

Soon afterwards we ran into a very light patch, with the wind dead ahead. I tacked *Belmore* offshore, and a few seconds later I saw that *Finisterre* and those close behind her had tacked the other way. My guess was wrong, and for a long time in typical Long Island calms we got the worst of local conditions. Eventually the wind came in again from a new direction, which favoured us well; we were lucky to finish ninth, some ninety seconds astern of *Finisterre* on corrected time; it was not a very good place, but I was delighted with the result, as it had shown that in the light conditions of the race *Belmore*'s handicap allowance, under the rating of the Cruising Club of America, was reasonable. *Finisterre* had to give us a handicap of some eight minutes for every hundred miles of the course and *Belmore* had showed she could go to windward without handicap, even if she had fallen back at the rate of ten minutes per hundred miles on the light-wind-spinnaker run. I was also pleased with the crew performance of *Belmore*, seen alongside first-rate American yachts; it was their brisk handling of the spinnaker under George that enabled me to cut inside at the leeward buoy.

The next race was to be George's. It was not that he was likely to need the practice of jockeying for a start, nor rounding a buoy, and I knew already that George had never skippered a yacht in a race, but it would be valuable for each mate-of-the-watch to gain confidence that comes from racing a boat successfully as skipper.

To give George unhampered responsibility for the race, over a similar course to the previous day, I asked Bobbie Lowein, whose *Danegeld* was again in company with us, if I could sail for the day with him. It would be a splendid chance to watch *Belmore* sailing from outside, besides the pleasure of sailing in such a fine yacht as *Danegeld*. And so it all came about.

Despite the logic of the case it was still quite a pull for me to hand over to someone else sole responsibility for a yacht entrusted to my charge; an accident then, whether due to her fault or that of any other yacht, might bring down to undignified failure the whole venture on which so much effort had been spent by the Royal Naval Sailing Association. So it was a great relief to me when I saw George keep well clear from the starting manœuvres, to cross the line quietly a couple of minutes after the first rush of keenly handled yachts, each with vast experience of racing starts behind them. He stood clear, too, at the first mark of the course, but otherwise handled the yacht really well in conditions that seemed to suit her. Mike Tanner was acting as mate, and through the binoculars I watched each sail-shift and spinnaker gybe without spotting a flaw in the organization.

That George should bring her in fourth in such company, three minutes astern of *Finisterre* on corrected time, was so satisfying to me that I felt certain it must also give him improved confidence.

Another day in Long Island Sound we spent becoming familiar with the life-saving equipment. First of all Roy, a very strong swimmer, showed the way by deliberately falling overboard in full oilskins as we sailed on a broad reach; when he had been picked up, the others in turn went over in their lifebelts to get the feel of it. 'Man overboard' is often practised with a lifebelt, which is easily picked up with a boat-hook on passing, but it is sometimes not realized how difficult it is to hoist on board a man whose oilskins are waterlogged. It was a good day for life-saving equipment, as later someone lurched heavily against the yacht's coated-wire lifeline, which parted where a splice had rusted unnoticed under its plastic coating; at sea in bad weather that failure could easily have cost a man his life, but in flat calm within Long Island Sound it merely warned that the lifelines should be renewed before the ocean race.

This happened when we were utterly becalmed. We had been invited to supper by Alf Loomis at his Huntington home, so laboriously *Belmore* crept towards Cold Spring Harbour towed by the dinghy, which each of us rowed for ten minutes at a time.

'I hope you don't expect us to cross the Atlantic this way, Skipper,' said Tim at the end of his stint. But a few weeks later as we lay becalmed hour after hour in the North Sea, within a couple of hundred miles of the finish of the Trans-atlantic race, it was Tim who bemoaned that dinghy towing was not allowed.

From Cold Spring Harbour we sailed at dawn. Out in Long Island Sound George came on deck to act as navigator for the passage to New London, which we sailed in bright clear conditions with a quiet breeze. Eight years before, in early June, I had made the same visit and sailed the same passage afterwards; then Alf Loomis came on board *Samuel Pepys* at anchor in a gale, and during the passage we lost our spinnaker boom when a squall struck the yacht around mid-night. Long Island Sound is not all calms and light airs.

This time *Belmore* had a quiet passage until George called me at 3 a.m. as he was steering her under spinnaker into the entrance of New London. Just past New London Ledge light-house, the wind died completely, and the tide took us slowly back towards the Sound, because I was reluctant to anchor in a main shipping channel. Then came a breeze from the north, but as we tacked up harbour the shore lights to the northward blotted out; soon we were enveloped in dense fog. We sailed towards the last seen street lamp until the soundings showed we were out of the big ship channel, then anchored some fifty yards from the unseen shore. With the dawn we felt our way along the last mile to Burr's Docks, tacking amongst a maze of moored yachts.

We all set off by car to visit Peter in hospital and found him still in bed, rather depressed at the continued pain in his back. However, his doctor encouraged me with a forecast that he had a good chance of being quite fit for the Bermuda race.

With eight days before the start I felt he would have to make a rapid recovery, and in the meantime adjusted the racing organization in my mind so that Peter would play a fuller part as navigator, and not be required for heavy work on deck. It was a bonus to the original plans that my own spinal injury had caused no trouble under a steadily increasing trial of deck work.

Meantime we were being helped out by a young Englishman, Bill Dean, who chanced to be in America on holiday, and for a whole week was a hard-working member of the crew of *Belmore*.

The next stage of training was our final race practice with a series of passage races organized by the Off Soundings Club. In these some 200 yachts gathered, and on each of two days raced to some different Long Island harbour where the whole fleet gathered in the evening as a community of well over a thousand keen sailing men and women. On the third day, private races or cruising passages took them back to their own harbours. For us in *Belmore* this was splendid sport and a thoroughly enjoyable sailing weekend, with the actual racing rather less intense than the previous weekend with the New York Yacht Club. The training plan aimed at further practice in delegated responsibilities, more than further sharpening of racing drill, and was designed also to give some relaxation in the tempo of training and preparation, so as to counter any tendency to staleness before the start of the Bermuda race.

For the first race, of some twenty-five miles to finish off Three-Mile Harbour, George was invited to race with Bobbie Lowein in *Danegeld*, so Mike was the mate in *Belmore* and Tim Sex became navigator and tactician. There were some fifty yachts in our class, but instead of picking some special rival to pace as we had done with *Finisterre* the previous weekend, I made a cruising start and followed our own course and plan. This was to give Mike practice in sail trimming and prepared evolutions, more than sudden sail shifts such as would be likely with any match racing against a special rival; it also gave Tim practice in navigation and long-distance tactics more than the cut-and-thrust tactics of round-the-buoy racing.

Again our luck was in, as the changing conditions throughout the day gave us exactly what suited us best. There was a light wind start, with full scope for sail-trimming and navigational accuracy across a brisk tidal stream; then later in the day the wind breezed up to a good twenty knots to give Mike practice in spinnaker handling in stiff conditions.

This turned out to be one of our most enjoyable races of the whole venture. The yacht was well tuned and sailed excellently, with an ample share of the fortune of the race; she achieved fifth place in her very large class. More important than this it showed me that Mike had a mastery over the sail trimming that was so vital for an ocean-racing mate-of-the-watch. A record was kept as usual, and from this it showed that minor slips while racing cost about three minutes twenty-five seconds, while the cruising start represented a further loss of thirteen seconds over a flat-out performance; it was a delightful sail, as planned, but those four odd minutes in an eight-hour race gave a reasonable indication of the difference between a well-trained crew racing really hard and the same crew doing well under relaxed conditions. A point that showed in almost any analysis of racing practice was that slips leading to delays were almost invariably due to a wandering of the attention from the job; commonest cause was chatter, and an approximate formula came out, without the more accurate analysis that a tape recorder might have allowed, that each non-essential word spoken on deck in a race cost one second to the yacht.

Often this would be a gross under-estimate, particularly if a crew was not so well trained; thus on the same Off Soundings race eight years before I remember pointing out generally to those on deck the unusual colour of the spinnaker of a yacht racing in another class; while we all looked at it a quick wind shift brought the breeze right ahead and I allowed the yacht to get in irons; caught unawares, the main sheet worker fumbled and got a riding turn on his winch which held the genoa back and somehow the runner got foul also. Four minutes and five yachts went by before *Samuel Pepys* was again sailing on her correct tack, her crew with two new bruises, one cut finger, and four irritated men. On that occasion the casual sentence 'Look at that colour' cost a minute for each word. Winning crews must needs be men of few words in their races.

Oddly enough that incident befell *Samuel Pepys* in almost the identical position off Gardiner's Island Ruins, where on that day ten years later we were to have our biggest racing slip in *Belmore*. She was running at about maximum speed under a straining spinnaker, whose pole was almost on the forestay. Astern of us was *Golliwog*, watching for any chance to get past us, but unable to do so as long as *Belmore*'s sails were trimmed to their best; Mike was watching just as closely, determined not to be caught out by the wind shifts that are notorious in that position. His order to haul aft the spinnaker sheet coincided with a comment by the sheetman on the cut of the *Golliwog*'s sail seen from ahead; few men can act with precision when talking, so the sheet took charge, the spinnaker fell in, and in a matter of seconds we could only note sadly the cut of the *Golliwog*'s sail seen from astern.

The next day was Mike's race as skipper over a similar course. Tim was to act as his mate on deck, with George as navigator; Mike particularly invited me to come although I took no part in the crew, and mostly I watched or photographed the race from the cabin. It was another good race, and I was delighted to see on Mike's face his complete lack of anxiety when another yacht among the crowd around us approached on a collision course close-hauled on the port tack, without apparently appreciating her responsibility to keep clear. Neither craft nor the weather will always obey the rules, and the good mate-of-the-watch needs to be able to retain command of the situation with confidence, such as Mike showed so clearly. That alone made this race really worth while, apart from the practice it gave to Tim in charge of the fore-deck and sail-trimming; *Belmore* also did well enough to gain seventh place in her large class, and after the finish we enjoyed sailing past the whalers in Green Port to anchor in Shelter Island's Dearing Harbour for the night.

Another race had been planned for the following day, but there was little enough wind in the early morning when Dr. Rozendaal brought his yacht *Katrina* beside *Belmore* and persuaded me to accept a tow while the tide was still in our favour. Once clear of Shelter Island the two yachts ran side by side under spinnaker past Plum Island, Great Gull Island, and through the Race, which lived up to its name with a good range of tidal eddies and small whirls. Meantime Hans Rozendaal had himself come on board *Belmore* to check through our medical stores and organization. This was the more welcome as Peter, who had taken over the medical equipment from a doctor in England, now seemed uncertain for our crew; it was most valuable to us all to have direct instructions from Hans on the equipment we carried. In many cases he replaced items of equipment with others which he felt would suit the needs of the yacht better, as only the previous year Hans had taken his *Katrina*, of a similar size to *Belmore*, on a cruise across the Atlantic; he knew at first hand what was best, and generously gave us this from his own medical supplies. He ensured that we all knew how to inject penicillin and he gave us ample supplies of this, in case anyone should suffer from appendicitis during the long races on our own. We were to be even more grateful for this before we reached England again.

Then, past Fisher's Island, *Katrina* took *Belmore* in tow as the wind failed at the entrance to Mystic; we were towed quietly past worn-out skeletons of old ships on the foreshore. In Mystic's shipyard *Belmore* was to be hauled out for the final rubbing down and painting of the bottom; to make it easier for us while the yacht was out of the water, Hans Rozendaal very generously lent us the use of his *Katrina* as a living-ship.

So on Monday, 13th June, with the Bermuda race due to start on the following Saturday afternoon, the *Belmore* was hauled out on a slipway, and at once the six of us got to work to rub down the bottom. While waiting for the high tide that was essential for this operation I rang up Peter's doctor for news. He still felt that Peter might be fit, but wanted another opinion, so asked for twenty-four hours more before the decision was made. That evening, with the *Belmore*'s bottom rubbed so smooth that the slightest breath should start her through the water when afloat, we were all picked up by Mr. Blunt White, the Chairman of the Transatlantic Race Committee, and one of our rivals in the Bermuda race. He had the same *White Mist*, which eight years before had beaten me by fifteen minutes, when she came second in the small class of the Bermuda race. We dined on a baron of beef so vast that it could have fed the entire order of Beefeaters, besides the dozen of us round the table.

Then with the dawn the six of us got to work painting on the anti-fouling coat that we hoped would keep her bottom smooth until the end of the Transatlantic race. The whole plan for the yacht's bottom had been worked out many months beforehand in conjunction with Rear-Admiral Boxer, who was an expert on underwater paints; the value of his advice was proved two months later when the yacht was hauled out in England with a completely clean bottom, which had a very large effect on her racing performance in light winds. With the last brush of paint on the under-surface of the keel the

9 Some of the yachts of Class A at the start of the Bermuda race. The yawl *Dyna* (A7 marked on sail) was the class winner and sailed on in the Transatlantic race

10 The yawl *Windigo* in Class A of the Bermuda race

11　The yawl *Stormy Weather* finished half-way up Class B in the Bermuda race, but crossed the line an hour and a half after *Belmore*. In 1935 she won the Transatlantic race to Norway, followed by a win in the Fastnet race, and next year was winner of the large class in the Bermuda race

12　The schooner *Fortune*, of Class B, and sloop *Cyane*, winner of Class C in the Bermuda race. *Cyane* also competed in the Transatlantic race

agreed time had come for my telephone call to Peter's doctor. I was worried about the verdict, not only because it would be a blow to the efficiency of our crew if he were not fit, but also because it would mean leaving one of us ill so far from home. But at least we would now get a definite decision, after waiting to the last possible moment in the hope of his coming with us.

Peter was not fit to sail.

It seemed almost impossible that with the Bermuda race due to start in four days' time any relief could get leave, fly out to New York and reach us at New Port; yet when the R.N.S.A. had already put so much into the venture I felt this was the right thing to suggest to those at home, and wrote out a cable giving the name of an R.N.S.A. member who I felt would best fit into the crew for this last-minute reorganization. It was Petty Officer Barrett, who was a permanent member of the crew of *Meon Maid*, the sister ship to *Belmore*; from his application to volunteer six months before I remembered that he was a bachelor with no special ties. He would be used to living in an identical yacht, almost certainly be immune to seasickness, and keen enough to join us.

I called an immediate meeting with the mates and we discussed the situation on the jetty. I knew there were many young American men keen for a berth in the long ocean races, but my instructions were that every effort should be made to fill any crew vacancies with members of the Association. Then there was Bill Dean, who was a member of the R.N.S.A. and might have been able to join our crew completely in spite of other plans.

After a full discussion of every point of view amongst us, I asked first for the opinion of the junior member. 'I think you should ask them at home, sir, for that petty officer we met at Cowes in the *Meon Maid*,' declared Mike Tanner.

'Bassett's his name, I think,' said George, 'and he's my

E

choice too. If they can get him, and if he can fly out in time; it will still be a hell of a job for him to get into our drill. But he looked the sort that might make it.'

So without any changes the scribbling on the scrap of paper in my pocket was dictated over the telephone as a cable.

6

Preparations for the Start

THE message was despatched asking that Petty Officer Barrett be flown out at once, and there were still arrangements to be made for the return to England of Peter Paffard, who was disabled in hospital. Several good friends, met since we arrived in America only three weeks earlier, promised to look after this. Peter would have seen America only from an ambulance and his hospital bed when we left, but at least there would be friends to assist him.

Before leaving we all set off with Major Smythe, the yard manager, to visit Mystic Seaport, a superb maritime museum in the form of an old whaling village, with many craft of historical interest lying at its wharfs or hauled out on the grass between the buildings. It was all intriguing, but somehow we moved steadily towards *Columbia*, the winner of the last America's Cup challenge, which was lying afloat in the seaport. By sheer chance we reached the *Columbia* in a group at the same time as another similar group; it was Bobbie Lowein and the crew of *Danegeld*, which had separated from *Belmore* after the Off Soundings races, to be hauled out for her bottom-cleaning at a boatyard some twenty miles away. *Danegeld* had then sailed into Mystic River, but we decided not to race the fifty-odd miles to Newport, as the need for the crew of *Belmore* at that stage was to relax the tension of intensive training.

Fog hid the bank half a mile away as *Belmore* set off alone, towed down the winding Mystic River by the helpful skipper of a motor launch; then we sailed out through Fisher's Island Sound, still in the fog, and tacked quietly for an hour or two before a slant in the wind allowed *Belmore* to overcome the fast-running stream of the Race by squeezing close inshore where the tide was slacker. It was intended as a restful passage, with no sail drills and no more effort than necessary to reach Newport.

In the afternoon the visibility cleared to nearly five miles as we sailed past places with the delightful-sounding names of Narragansett Bay and Quonochontaug. On the radio we heard many ships report 'nil visibility' ahead and to the south; one ship, fitted with radar, was faced with the same passage into Block Island Sound that we had forced in dense fog due to Peter's injured back on making America. She reported that she would remain at sea until conditions improved for the approach to the channel.

We ran into dense fog after dark when a mile or two south of Port Judith; around us were the sounds of several craft feeling their way into the harbour. I stayed below most of the time, plotting the progress of the yacht and noting carefully the reaction of each mate-of-the-watch in these rather difficult conditions. It was reassuring to sense the quiet alertness they showed; when the position of an unseen ship was doubtful as she approached from somewhere ahead, then the genoa was lowered quietly to reduce speed in the moderate swell; this cut down the noise of our bow slapping into the water; it made it easier to judge the direction of a syren, and to pick up the burr of a diesel engine as a ship came closer. Once the danger was past up went the genoa with quiet efficiency.

In the early hours of Thursday, 16th June, *Belmore* felt her way through the fog to an anchorage off the Ida Lewis Yacht Club in Newport Harbour, Rhode Island. With the morning light we found ourselves on the fringe of a great fleet of yachts anchored ready for the start of the Bermuda race in two days' time. It was a relief to have safely reached the starting place after several thousand miles of voyaging; there had been so many chances of accident that could have made *Belmore* a non-starter.

I was confident of a creditable performance whatever happened over the final crew man; yet the very progress we had made reflected back anxiety because it was obvious that the yacht, her tuning, and her crew-training gave her the best chance of winning the Bermuda race that had ever come to a British yacht in the fifty years' history of this premier classic of ocean-racing events. Complete success was within her reach. It seemed most unlikely to me that Petty Officer Barrett, with his naval duties to be reorganized, could reach us in time for the Bermuda race, and I suddenly had a flash of inspiration that a drastic change might give *Belmore* the best chance. John Illingworth had helped to design and build her, besides skippering her into third place in the last Bermuda race, so might not he be the key to her winning? He was a man to fly round the world at five minutes' notice, and was certainly Britain's most experienced ocean-racing skipper.

Although none of us had ever sailed in a yacht with him before, I felt that he would be able to blend his ocean-racing genius to the highly tuned organization that I had built. I felt perfectly entitled to act on my own behalf in this change; it would not conflict with my orders to take command of the yacht for the venture if someone else should skipper her for one race while I acted in some other capacity onboard.

Only the day before, I had consulted my mates in *Belmore* over making up the shortage in the crew, and so close after that it would seem a slap in the eye if I made a much more drastic change without consultation, for which there was no time. It did not worry me that Barrett might already be on the way, which in fact was the case, as an extra man would be possible should they both arrive onboard. But the difficulties became more obvious when I sat in the cable office scribbling out drafts of my message. For one thing I had no idea where John Illingworth might be at that moment, so I went to find a yachtsman who was often in touch with him.

'John is up to the neck in organizing the sail-training race,' he said. 'He'd probably drop everything and come, but it's not fair to him and not fair to you either. You've got a good chance of winning yourself.'

So the whole idea was thrown over the side and for some time forgotten. Yet with the events as they happened laid out as exhibits to the case, it is a nice exercise to surmise how *Belmore* would have fared in 1960 with John Illingworth as skipper and Erroll Bruce as navigator. Better, I think, and perhaps Erroll Bruce would have been fresher to skipper her in the Transatlantic race that followed.

There was an enormous amount to be done before the start, as well as the decision on who should crew *Belmore*. Only those who have managed races abroad can realize the weight of administrative requirements, both by the race authorities and also the officials concerned with the business of any vessel moving from one country to another. All were helpful, and that certainly included Walter Dring, whose personality as the Customs officer is well known to generations of British yachtsmen who have entered or cleared at Newport. Yet Walter Dring had to point out it would all be so much easier when I knew who my crew was to be: if the man is doubtfully in mid-air on the way over, he insisted, it is wrong to complete the formalities that give him permission to leave the country, even with an inventive guess in quintuplet at his Christian names, age, town of birth, and family history. Yet he needed the forms to be completed at once.

'Can't your secretary deal with that?' suggested Walter,

when he noticed that my answers to the third copy of some form had wandered a bit from the original.

But each one of us in the crew was busy, so I kept up a succession of vigorous rushes from office to office by taxi, by dinghy, and by sheer foot-slogging.

Belmore had on board a great deal of equipment that was not necessary for the race to Bermuda. We had left Bermuda for a two-months' cruise with sufficient food, spare equipment, and repair gear to be entirely self-dependent if needed, except for slipping. But less than half the food had been eaten, few of the repairs had been necessary, and in many cases we had been given things in America that made other gear redundant. Much of this got in our way, so we planned to ask the U.S. Navy to help, as we knew that unwanted equipment from the Annapolis yachts would be transferred to their escorting warship. Colonel Ferguson showed us the way to everything we needed, and it is somehow rather typical of the sport of ocean-racing that an American colonel should give vigorous help to enable British sailors on leave to be assisted by the United States Navy; certainly all went very well, and *Belmore* was invited to join the American Academy yachts at a naval pier; soon afterwards the captain and executive officer of U.S.S. *Hank* came onboard the *Belmore* to return my call. Within a few minutes five hundredweight of gear was ready for transfer to the destroyer. The last tin of surplus ox tongue was accompanying my typewriter on to the jetty as a cable was handed onboard.

'Petty Officer Barrett will join you at Newport.'

This message stirred us like a squall in the doldrums. Hour by hour it had seemed less likely that our request for Barrett could have been granted. The short message showed each of us the strength of our support in England; vigorous and decisive action must have been taken by someone to get so swift and favourable a result.

'George,' I said, when we had read the cable together, 'we are going to win this Bermuda race.'

'If you say so, sir, we ruddy well will,' he answered.

After many weeks of intensive training, nerves may be taut-stretched before an important race; jubilation can be as dangerous as depression, especially when dealing with situations which are outside the training of habit. Eight years before on the eve of another Bermuda race-start, when *Samuel Pepys* had come alongside a jetty at Newport for final unloading of surplus gear in just the same way, I had bungled sailing from the jetty due to excess of confidence, and put her aground with a falling tide. Only immediate help by John Nicholas Brown, owner of a rival yacht which we were to beat on handicap after she had finished the course in a very fast time, saved the yacht I then commanded from injury that might have put her out of the race.

Leaving the jetty in *Belmore* presented the similar problem of a brisk wind from ahead, and little sea-room until clear. This time I was determined to apply the lesson of the past by waiting for the assistance of a motor-launch to tow us clear of the jetty.

Somehow the motor-boat got out of control and fell across the wind when we had been towed a few feet clear of the jetty. When the motor-boat went ahead again, at the angle to which she had drifted, *Belmore*'s stern would inevitably swing on to a pile from which a jagged bolt projected a few inches above the water-line. To strike this at even one knot would be enough to pierce the hull and put us out of the race, so I ordered the tow to be let go; those on the fore-deck were facing the towing motor-boat and saw no reason for the order, so felt I meant something else, while the crew of the motor-launch could not see the danger, as *Belmore* obscured their view. When my order was repeated it was expressed with such fury that everyone within a hundred yards knew all about it, but still only those of us aft in the yacht had seen the reason.

We hoisted the mainsail without further trouble and sailed clear with a crew downcast by such public censure. 'Oh, for the ability,' I mused, as I kicked myself, 'to foresee every situation so precisely that it should never be necessary to shout.'

Next morning when we woke up at anchor off the Ida Lewis Yacht Club a square-shouldered man with bright eyes and a red beard under a partly bald head helped to cook breakfast as though it was the most natural thing in the world. Two days before Petty Officer Barrett was onboard *Meon Maid* in Portsmouth Harbour preparing her for a race when a message came asking if he was willing to join *Belmore* in America; he finished the splice he was tucking, packed his sailing kit, sold his motor-bicycle, and set off for the airport to be flown across the Atlantic. It was his first visit to America, but without bother he caught a train for the journey to New Port and then found his way to the Ida Lewis Yacht Club around midnight. He sighted *Belmore*'s dinghy, with a note left in it to explain where she lay in the fog among the other hundred or so yachts; he rowed off and found us asleep, so crept into the vacant bunk and went to sleep himself.

After breakfast I checked point by point through his experience and his equipment; it was just what I had hoped for, and his arrival without any fuss showed him to be the adaptable man we needed. Barry was popular at once; he was immediately one of the team and as much at home as though he had known each one of us for years. 'But I haven't done steering, sir, and I must get some oilskins', at once made clear any limitations.

We set sail for a few hours of drill; it was the only chance for Barry to see anything of our methods before the race itself. The fog was thick as we tacked, set, and re-set spinnakers, gybed or re-gybed within Newport Harbour. Several other yachts were also at sail drill, unseen save for an occasional glimpse through the fog; they were not those yachts whose scratch crews might need some practice before the race, but *Finisterre*, *Carina*, *Cyane*, *Rhubarb*, and others of the first team, whose performance we already knew to be superb. Whoever won that race was going to deserve it.

Ashore on the evening before the start a meeting of skippers was held for final briefing by members of the sailing committee, captains of the escorting ships, and experts on navigational aids, meteorology, and the Gulf Stream. This last was particularly interesting, as seven sail crossings of the Gulf Stream had shown me that any idiosyncrasies from its general easterly progress were of vital importance in this race.

Alf Loomis, an ocean-racing navigator of unrivalled experience and a rival in this race, gave me valuable advice on the yachtsman's application to what the expert had told us all. Just before the meeting Carleton Mitchell had invited me to see all he had onboard *Finisterre*, and also willingly gave valuable advice on each point I asked him. His masterly handling of each subject, and the preparation of his yacht, certainly made clear enough that *Finisterre* was the yacht we must beat to win. Handicap allowances for the race were published at this meeting; *Belmore* was given two hours less than for her race in 1959. Relative to the six yachts entered in both races, and nearest in handicap to *Belmore*, her allowance was forty-nine minutes down.

'It's said that you take this race very seriously,' suggested a pressman who caught me after the meeting. 'Do you think your yacht has a chance when no foreign yacht has ever won before?'

'I have not come here just to eat the good food and see the pretty girls,' I answered. 'My object is to win. Perhaps 134 other skippers have the same object though.'

'What are the chances of an English win?'

'There are three English yachts out of a total of 135, so I suppose the chances work out at about forty to one,' was really the best answer I could give.

'Which English yacht has the best chance?'

'*Belmore*,' I answered, 'as her crew have had the opportunity to work together longest.'

'It's been suggested on the waterfront that they are rather inexperienced in this sort of racing.'

'I helped to choose them,' I replied, 'and I'll wait for my answer until after this race and the Transatlantic race too.'

'You say that *Belmore* has the best chance of winning. What weather conditions would suit her best?'

'Fog at the start with light head winds; lots of squalls in the Gulf Stream, and a gale somewhere,' which was my opinion. 'These are the three points on which our crew-training has concentrated. We don't want light wind running.'

'But everyone has told us that a gale will help the big yachts.'

'I don't agree,' I retorted. 'Small yachts have stronger crews in proportion to their sail area, and it's easier to train a very good small crew than a very good large one.'

'But what about the fine equipment in the large yachts? Doesn't that give them a big advantage in bad weather?'

'Some small yachts are well-equipped for hard-weather racing, and in any case if the weather is hard then it's the crew that matter most.'

Clearly the support for small yachts in a gale was considered to be a joke, and I noticed Richard Nye, owner of *Carina*, coming our way.

'Well, ask Mr. Nye,' I suggested. 'He'll probably be the winner of the Transatlantic race.'

'Just one last question, please. Have you any special tactics for the Bermuda race, or is that secret?'

'Nothing is secret in *Belmore*, nor our rivals either, so far as

I've seen. My tactics are to win the small yacht class, and that will almost certainly mean the Bermuda Trophy as well.'

If tactics mean the geographical movement of the craft, then that answer was all that could be given for a race from one point in the ocean to another one 640 miles away. The yacht would be deployed so that wind and current would take her as fast as possible to her destination. But if tactics mean also the handling of the crew, then our whole period of preparation and training had gone towards a complex organization intended to get the best out of each man over a period of just over five days.

In fact, I had planned on the precise racing time of five days and four hours, and within that period practised with the crew everything that I felt might happen in the yacht. The voyage over the course in reverse had shown that the crew of *Belmore*, however fit, definitely tired after two nights at sea, to the extent of minds working more slowly and determination falling; it was likely that most of our rivals would have a similar problem, and perhaps many would have it more acutely than us, as their crews had experienced less intense training together than we had enjoyed. It is my belief that the Bermuda race is usually won during the third and subsequent nights at sea; and it is often lost, particularly by young crews, from over-excitement on the first two days.

It was going to be a slow race and *Belmore* had a young crew; except for the skipper, nearing fifty, all were in their physical prime of twenty-four to thirty years old. The plan was to start with the emotional temperature, which controls the output of energy, as near normal as possible, breaking down quickly into a watch routine to which all were accustomed. I reckoned it might be the third night before we were well into the Gulf Stream, so until then it would be alert watch-racing without any supercharge pressure.

Navigation would be of special importance in the early

part of the race to vector the yacht into the Gulf Stream meander perhaps two days after the start. The whole pattern seemed to point that as Peter had dropped out, the skipper should undertake the navigation as far as the Gulf Stream; this would require full-time effort and thereby divert the skipper's energies, leaving the mates-of-watches to make quiet progress without calling on reserves of energy. It was my intention that after forty-eight hours of racing the yacht should be reasonably well placed, but with crew fresh enough to keep her sailing really well through squalls or rough weather; the key, if my hopes of some hard weather came true, would be the ability to pile on sail quickly as conditions eased after a blow. I planned to hand on the navigational work after the Gulf Stream, and put on the boost pressure of hard sailing during the last nights.

Going back onboard *Belmore*, as she lay at anchor among a fleet of fine yachts, I felt confident that we now had a yacht fully equipped, a crew fully prepared, with a plan to suit them. All we needed more was ample luck, without which few races are ever won, when the competition is so hot.

'Hi! Wait for me!'

7

The Bermuda Race

SATURDAY, 18th June, proved as foggy as the forecast had foretold. At least one skipper was satisfied, not because it showed the weather men were right, but because the conditions were splendid for his plan; I hoped that in many rival yachts the crews would find the conditions difficult for the start and that they might spend long hours with eyes straining through the darkness when crossing the main shipping routes. It was an unfriendly thought, perhaps, towards those who had so kindly cared for us in America, but this was to be a hard-fought race and I felt that the more trials it offered that came within the training of my crew the better was our chance.

There was scarcely enough wind to sail out of harbour, and a yacht tacking out to the start would have been an infernal nuisance to the 135 other competitors, all quietly motoring out in line ahead, besides the hundreds of spectator craft and the dozen or more Coast Guard vessels that were to shepherd them off the course. For the first mile Colonel Ferguson and his son towed us in their outboard motor-boat, then *Carina* came up and took over the tow. In my last Bermuda race, eight years before, Dick Nye in his former *Carina* had won the class in which the yacht I skippered came third, and he had won the Bermuda trophy that year as well; before that the main trophy had only twice gone outside the large class in the eleven races when smaller yachts had been separated in class.

Through the gloom *Carina* took us close up to the Brenton Reef Light Vessel, which formed one end of our line, then over to the anchored Coast Guard ship which formed the other end. Each of the five classes were due to start at intervals of a quarter of an hour, with the largest in a few minutes' time; but as we passed there was a broadcast hail that the start had been postponed in case the fog cleared later. 'It won't,' shouted Dick Nye. 'It will get thicker.' He was right.

There was nothing to be done, so George lay on his bunk below decks while *Carina* jogged along twining her way through the yachts, motor-launches, tugs, pleasure steamers, and multitude of other craft; once a great form loomed up ahead and there was a splash and rattle as a large merchant ship anchored. George switched on the radio for the relaxing power of music, but the local stations kept breaking through with reports on the Bermuda-race start.

And that is how we got the first news that Class A were starting. George shot up the hatch and shouted out to *Carina*: 'Class A warning signal is up.'

'Thanks,' said Dick Nye without concern. 'I'll take you back a little closer to the start and then cast off for my own start in Class B.'

Dick Nye would certainly not be put off by the fog, and as we watched yachts from each class in turn manœuvre for their starts it was interesting to see that many were handled with as much dash as though all the hundreds of craft that dotted the area, unseen, were clearly visible.

When our turn came, 105 yachts had already set off on the race in the four classes ahead of us, yet the sea seemed just as crowded as the various spectator craft moved in the closer to see some of the fun. The fog was also thicker, and after sailing under the stern of the Coast Guard ship used as committee vessel we lost sight of her astern after one minute forty-five seconds, and it took the same time before we sighted the light-vessel ahead; that meant we could see about one-third of the length of the starting-line, and as there were thirty-one yachts in our class many would get a foul wind if they hugged the committee ship to see the starting signals. However, the radio commentator always broadcast news of starting signals, and the radio beacon on the light-ship gave us her bearing, so it seemed best to try a start in the middle of the line, out of sight of either end. We assumed that the committee would guard the line with radar, and any yacht over at the start would lose the time before a Coast Guard boat would recall her, as well as the delay in turning back; but this seemed a reasonable risk in order to get a clear wind, which was then blowing at eight knots, making a close fetch of our course to Bermuda.

Several other yachts had the same idea at the start, and we found ourselves among a bunch of the best ones, all out of sight of the ships marking the line ends. *Danegeld* made a fast start some distance ahead of us, without using the radio beacon, and, on sighting the bows of the light-vessel soon afterwards, decided that she might have been over the line, so turned back to correct her start.

We were away, sailing close-hauled on the starboard tack in conditions that normally suited *Belmore* well. Yet she was somehow not in her stride. It was important to my mind to get the crew rhythm right, so within five minutes of crossing the starting-line I ordered watch-racing, and myself went below, hoping those off watch would soon follow. After a few minutes below the feeling came that she was trimmed stern-heavy, so I moved a few sail bags further forward and myself climbed right forward below the deck.

'Any better?' I asked Mike at the tiller.

'I think so,' he answered. '*Doncherry* is still fifty yards ahead. 'It's so hard to tell in the fog.'

Certainly her trim had been changed slightly, but I think

13 The yawl *Windrose* in Class D of the Bermuda race; she was second on
corrected time in the Transatlantic race

14 *Belmore* running before a light wind through a quiet sea in the Bermuda race; her weakest point again yawls

it was that the sea frequency had not suited her at the start; as the waves slowly changed the feeling of uneasiness in her motion soon disappeared. Four hours after the start we sailed into a patch clear of fog; it was like coming from a dense forest into a glade with a herd of deer. Twenty-eight yards were in sight, all but two to leeward, and with about as many abaft the beam as before it.

'She's doing well,' I told George. 'All give us time on handicap except two, and there's *Danegeld* well abaft the beam as one of them.'

But things were so quiet that it all seemed rather an anti-climax for the Bermuda race to which so much of our efforts had been aimed; there was no excitement, no waves, little wind, no tacking, and no sail-shifting. Perhaps my efforts at lowering emotional temperature to reduce expenditure of energy had gone too far. During the middle watch the wind freed and the spinnaker went up as our first sail-shift; but the time of this shift put it in the class of a slow cruising drill. Then when the next watch took over they had to gybe at once, which always gives a hint that the yacht may have been sailing by the lee for some time.

Again the weather helped. The wind lightened and shifted several times with a renewal of thicker fog, so on the second day there were fifteen sail-shifts; still no hectic rushes, but enough to keep things alive for the watches. The work was uneven; three sail-shifts in one watch's middle, forenoon, and dogs to the twelve shifts the other watch carried out in their morning, afternoon, and first; but so were the conditions uneven.

Standing four-hour watches were kept throughout the race, with Mike and Tim as a very strong team doing the morning, afternoon, and first. Opposite to them was George, assisted by Roy, while Barry, our new arrival, was permanent cook and always on call from the deck if needed. By night the

F

first call for an extra hand on deck was answered by the skipper, who took the tiller for most evolutions, but by day it was the cook who answered the first call, unless actually cooking a meal, when the skipper went on deck instead.

After the second night the visibility improved enough for a sight of the horizon, and navigational activity became intensive. We were making for a position to meet the forecast meander of the Gulf Stream, and in such light following winds it was important to reach this at the northern point of its turn so as to get the full benefit in the swirl of the current until it reached its southern turning point. As soon as a clear horizon allowed sights to establish our position we altered course thirty degrees to port at a speed of only three knots. *Pandora V* was the first yacht we identified in the improved visibility; she was in Class B, which had started three-quarters of an hour before us, and gave *Belmore* a handsome time allowance; this was encouraging. Then the visibility closed down to a couple of miles.

We were some twenty miles short of the expected first contact with the Gulf Stream current, so from then on each hour a sight of the sun was taken with the eye only three feet above sea level; at this height the horizon is less than two miles away, which was just inside the visibility distance. Immediately after the sight a radio count of the Consol numbers was made; then the canvas bucket went over the stern for a sample of sea water to read the sea temperature; finally, in this hourly routine, came a visit up the mast to the lower spreaders for a better view of any signs of the stream on the surface of the ocean, lines of Sargasso weed, Portuguese Men-o'-War, or any swirl on the water. Each reading was recorded, and plotted on a graph; then the sight was worked out to give a single position line at right angles to the bearing of the sun.

Half an hour after noon, adjusted to zone plus three to give us daylight for washing up the evening meal, we met the Stream. In such calm weather I had expected to see a tide swirl on the edge, but either I missed this when calculating a sight below or none was visible. Mike sensed it as mate-of-the-watch, and the next hourly readings confirmed it, first by an increase of sea temperature, then by a change in the Consol count of dots and dashes; we were certainly being set eastwards and were probably within the northern curl of the meander, so I ordered the course to be changed twenty degrees to starboard in an effort to gain the centre of the moving stream.

From then on the multiple readings and calculations were made every half-hour; it was an almost continuous process of navigational work, leaving the sailing of the yacht entirely to each mate-of-the-watch. The next hour confirmed with certainty that we were in the Stream, and being carried to the south-east towards Bermuda; the fix from the sun and Consol showed a seven-mile advance in the hour, with no more than two knots from her speed through the water. I suspected the accuracy of my navigation, but the following hour showed another seven-mile advance; so did the one afterwards. Two yachts about three miles on the port beam as we entered the Stream had dropped out of sight astern, and for the next few hours none were in sight. Then, around 4 p.m. by our time, the visibility improved and eleven yachts were in sight around us; there was no time for me to check identities, except for *Soprano*, which crossed a hundred yards ahead; she was near the top rating of our Class E, so was another encouragement after two days of racing; but I had no time for anything but navigation, and to note that she was steering a course some thirty degrees different from *Belmore*. The wind we felt was south-south-west at four knots, but our tidal speed of five knots towards the south-south-east had brought this relative wind round from its true direction of north-west; those yachts not enjoying the push of the Gulf Stream would at least get more help from the wind as compensation, but on balance we were certainly doing much better in mid-current.

As the sun set I climbed to the upper spreaders and counted twenty-two yachts in sight; obviously a high proportion of the fleet had aimed for the same position as *Belmore*; we could identify none of them, except to know that *Danegeld* was not amongst them, but the sight was quietly encouraging for a yacht with the third lowest handicap of the whole fleet, when I had felt that we might have taken the first two days too easily.

At dusk the stars showed that we had been set by the Stream twenty-four miles in a direction of 150 degrees; this was practically straight for Bermuda and even if every other yacht got the same set it would increase the value of our handicap by reducing the effective length of the course.

Through the night, once the horizon was no longer visible, sights could not be taken; but each hour I took the count of the Consol readings and plotted these with the sea temperature. Around midnight I felt we must be clear of the Stream, and the increase of wind to ten knots suggested we were in still water; but it was three hours later that the Consol counts showed a sudden change from dots to dashes as we were set eastwards on the bottom arc of the meander. We altered course thirty degrees to starboard to clear the rush of the Stream, and soon afterwards dawn sights showed that in eighteen hours we had been carried by the Stream seventy-one miles to shorten the Bermuda-race course by 12 per cent of its total length.

We were spewed out amongst a host of yachts; from the look of it they had not all gained the same benefit as *Belmore*. We recognized *Siskiwit*, near the top rating of Class D, but too wild an optimism was brought back to sea level when we made out *Rhubarb* on our beam; she was six places above us in the rating list, and would give *Belmore* only seventy-five minutes of handicap over the whole course

So this was the time to put on the pressure, and I stirred

up the feeling that, come what may, we must keep on the tail of *Rhubarb*, which became our pace horse. At 1600 hours she was on the port bow one mile off by sextant angle, and twenty-four other yachts were in sight all round; by the end of the first watch on Monday, 21st June, *Belmore* had crept up to a hundred yards from her beam as we hoisted the spinnaker. From the anticlimax of three nights before, the race was becoming for us intensely exciting, although the sea had boasted waves no higher than one foot and the wind had never exceeded ten knots.

During that middle watch George was on his toes every second, taking turns with Roy to trim sails while the other steered; to get the best from her it really needed three men on deck, and I gave up navigation to assist a good deal of the time. The weather was unsettled, with occasional drizzle, and I had that feeling of apprehension that squalls were not far away. Around 3 a.m. a big yawl worked her way past us in the darkness; her watch on deck were striving every yard of the way, and by her sail-trimmer's torch I caught sight in the binoculars of the number 477; it was *Mistral* of Class D, next in rating above *Siskiwit*, which we had sighted nearby the previous forenoon.

We were doing well enough, but a flaw in my crew plan began to affect us, and I did not appreciate it at once. The whole scheme of steady pressure by the watches during the first two days had worked out well, but I had not appreciated sufficiently the enormous load that would go into intense enough navigation to gain the best of the Gulf Stream; and I was now using myself as the boost pressure on top of that. Up to that time the log readings, taken every hour of the day and night, showed in my handwriting, except for the four hours of Monday afternoon when I had been so intent on half-hour plots that Mike had filled in the ship's log himself as mate-of-the-watch. This meant that since the race started four days before I had been awake during every hour, although I had got some sleep in periods of less than one hour.

My enthusiasm was still intense, but my tolerance was reduced. During the middle watch I came on deck when I saw a squall-cloud close astern; and at that moment things were unseamanlike with both runners unrove and lashed to the rigging, two genoas set at once, and a halyard foul. The squall brought rain without increase in wind, but in the meantime quite a little gale had blown on deck until I was satisfied that the yacht was again in sea-going trim ready for any surprises of that area.

My judgement suffered too, as next time I came up from writing the log-book we were hemmed in between *Mistral* and another yacht to leeward; *Belmore* was so placed that she could not overtake, her wind was foul, and in the case of an unseen squall she had no room for manoeuvre. Instead of telling the mate-of-the-watch to lower the genoa for a minute to drop under the stern of *Mistral*, I took over the tiller impatiently and gybed round in a tight circle to clear her; it was some minutes before George got the yacht going well again in the light easterly wind. I was angry and it was not a good thing.

At 4 a.m. George came below when his watch was relieved on deck. '*Mistral* is now astern, sir,' he reported, and I knew he meant also to imply 'and what's more, we've been sailing ruddy well.' He had, because *Mistral* was a very much bigger yacht.

'Well done,' I said, 'but I'm suspicious of squalls in this area.' However, I took in George's point and realized belatedly that I was getting over-tired.

'Mike,' I said, going on deck, 'damn the star-sights. I want to sleep until breakfast-time. Keep cracking, and use Barry unless you want me badly.'

So I had an undisturbed four hours of sleep and went on deck in light rain to see *Marvula* nearby; she was near the top rating of Class C, and there was the Swedish *Casella*, eighteen places above *Belmore* in the rating list, coming up astern. The wind had headed and we were unable to make our course for Bermuda. On the next tack we crossed *Golliwog* and *Pipe Dream*, both hot rivals in our class, and well worth making our targets for the day.

That afternoon I slept again for three hours, ignoring any chance of a sight should the drizzle lift. We had 180 miles to go at noon, so I tuned in to the special radio forecast for the race to get some news of the conditions to be expected for our landfall. 'No change since the last report. No strong winds expected,' came the forecast.

We had not received the last report, or any of the previous ones, but I made a joke of the second part, which was unfavourable to my plans.

'I badly want a gale, and as the forecast says there won't be one there is quite a reasonable chance that it will come. But a sight first would be best, as we've nothing since last night to go on.'

We still had the help of the Consolan, 450 miles to the northwards, whose signal came through clearly as I made a treble check count below.

'Good omen for your ruddy gale, sir,' George sung down the hatch. '*Stormy Weather* has just passed under our stern.'

Stormy Weather was high up in Class B, which class she had won only six years before, apart from her famous victories in the Transatlantic race, Bermuda race, and Fastnet race before the war; it seemed astonishing that little *Belmore* should be tacking ahead of her with less than a quarter of the course to go.

'That makes the gale almost a certainty, George,' I said with a wave of confidence. 'It's splendid, and if only I knew where *Finisterre* was I'd tell you also who will get the Bermuda trophy.'

Half an hour later a squall struck with a twenty-five knot wind. We had a double head-sail shift, first down to the R.O.R.C. and then down to the worker, followed by one roll in the main; a few minutes later we were back to full main and C.C.A. genoa. *Stormy Weather* and several other un-identified yachts had fallen well back astern. Things were livening up superbly; those seven hours of sleep were a godsend and I was on the fore-deck for each of the sail changes.

'Gale in the night would be perfect,' I prayed out loud, 'and then a clearing for sights well before the landfall.'

'Winning's not good enough,' said George. 'I want to be first home as well.' As the gale blew up we were all on the top of the world.

Around 10 p.m. a harder squall met us; around thirty knots, I estimated, but there was no time to bother too much about exact wind speeds as I went forward with Tim for a shift to the R.O.R.C. genoa; we then took in a couple of rolls. That lasted only a short time before we changed down again and took in two further rolls; *Belmore* was sailing superbly, and among the rain and the lightning I saw the lights of half a dozen yachts drop astern.

By midnight the barometer had dropped smartly and seemed set to go lower, so I was rather surprised when the wind eased soon afterwards; almost simultaneously we wound out a couple of rolls, with a headsail change back to genoa.

This was a premature move, and five minutes later it was blowing really hard with a wind shift; after plotting the wind direction on the chart I told George to come round on to the port tack, steering south by west. The rolls had gone back into the mainsail by then, making a total of seven, and Barry was on deck to back up with the work. Again I noticed more lights dropping astern, and it seemed that *Belmore* was rampaging past some really big yachts. In pouring rain we sailed close past two running before the wind, apparently without mainsails hoisted.

I was beginning to have a few apprehensions about the risk of hitting someone when suddenly the sails flapped and she was taken aback.

'What on earth are you doing?' I stormed at Roy on the tiller in this lull in the wind.

'I can't make out, sir,' he answered.

We had sailed from a gale into a near-calm patch; the wind came again from a direction seven points different. It came harder than we'd had before that night. *Belmore* heeled far over with the lee-side deck well awash; the sea was still not really rough but she was dragging through the water and difficult to control, which was not too safe considering the number of yachts that kept appearing close up through the spray and rain.

'We'll have the other watch up in oilskins,' I told George, 'and then put the trysail on her.'

It seemed the devil of a time while the watch below woke up and struggled into oilskins; they had not really been to sleep since turning in at midnight, but every movement was difficult when the yacht was being thrown around on her side. We had too much sail up, and I was impatient to get it off before we ran into some yacht hove-to.

When the main halyard was let go it went with a run. *Belmore* had no topping lift fitted, the main boom was sheeted hard in, and the skipper at the tiller was leaning under it to peer at a red light that had just winked over a wave-top on the lee-side. So the next thing I remembered in the darkness was Mike bundling me out of the way so that he could lash down in the cockpit the after end of the main boom; it had bounced on my head before making a quarter-inch dent in a cockpit-locker lid. However, I was still steering, and the red light to leeward was abaft the beam.

'Ready for the trysail,' reported Mike as he secured the last tyre round the mainsail.

'Wait,' I ordered, 'we are going fast enough.'

Mike seemed rather surprised by this and asked me how she was heading. With the wind shift she was almost making the course for Bermuda, and the speed log showed nearly six knots.

'Take her for a moment,' I said. 'I want to check the course below.'

It was not easy to get below at a big angle of heel, with the main boom lashed down close over the hatch; then wet clothes had to be stripped off before pulling out the chart. We were doing well on that course, and I did not mind getting to the eastwards as I felt certain that the wind would go round to south-west after the blow. Down below the motion was more apparent than on deck; she was pounding so violently that it was hard to avoid being thrown around. She was out of step with the waves, and each pitch was bigger than the last until a terrific crash brought her up all standing; then the whole process would start again.

'If I get the trysail on her,' I mused, 'it will be the heck of a pull to drag out a tired crew later to shift to the main. Without the trysail we will be inclined to hoist the main the sooner.'

Back on deck I felt that the wind had eased a trifle. Dawn was not far ahead, but meantime the light of another yacht reminded me of the collision danger so long as the darkness joined with the spray to obscure visibility.

'Stow the trysail below again,' I ordered. 'Carry on watch-racing. We'll have the mainsail on her again before long.'

Actually an hour and forty minutes went by with no sail hoisted abaft the mast. It was dawn by that time, and after all it was the trysail that I ordered to be hoisted.

There was no longer any fear of collision, but it seemed to me at the time that the trysail was all that the yacht could safely carry in those conditions.

It was the seas that kept *Belmore* under trysail until the main sail was set with seven rolls nearly five and a half hours after it had been lowered. The waves were not particularly high for a gale, perhaps twelve to thirteen feet was the mean wave height, but the frequency was such that above a certain speed she got into a rhythmic pitch, building up each time to an infernal crash; so I kept her down to this speed to avoid damage to the hull. Some waves were well above the average height, and even at four and a half knots she twice fell off a wave-top to crash some fifteen feet into the trough, landing as though she had been dropped on to a concrete jetty. Each time she stopped dead, quivering as though she had had enough.

At the second bad bump I was below and saw a spurt of water shoot up to the deckhead under the mast. Mike and I rushed to pull up the cabin sole, expecting to find the seams had opened up, but Mike was soon satisfied that there was nothing drastically wrong; with so much water about it was difficult to know where it came from, so we assumed that there was some leakage through the seams, but nothing beyond the capacity of our bilge pumps.

The Henderson pumps were very efficient, but we had to work at them about every half-hour to keep the water out of the upper bunks as she lurched to leeward; our clothes lockers were all flooded, but each man had packed every change of clothes in a separate polythene bag to guard against this very situation. We found later that the seams had not opened up, and probably at no time was the weight of water below very great, yet the motion was so violent that the water which found its way below as the waves washed over the deck was putting in a great deal of work to make it seem much more than it really was. A bucket of water hurled at the deck-head, to ricochet all over the cabin, seems a great deal more than the same bucketful wallowing quietly in the bilges.

Quite often the coachhouse ports on the lee side were under water as she lurched on the steep face of a wave; however, the average heel in the gusts was no more than fifty degrees when measured on the chart-table bulkhead. Fifty degrees is ample to make life difficult below, and when combined with an occasional flight to the deckhead, besides an intermittent shower-bath, sleep for those off watch is not really practicable. Somehow Barry managed to serve regular meals at the routine times; my navigating position was to leeward of the galley stove, so I was grateful for Roy's idea of asbestos string with which the kettle and cooking-pots were secured to the stove; the gymbals allowed for the heel, but it needed a good stout lashing to prevent the kettle taking flight when the yacht fell off a wave-top.

Plotting was difficult enough in any case. A canvas webbing belt held the navigator in line with the chart-table, placed athwartships across the foot of a quarter berth on which he sat to work; but this belt did not stop movement up and down, so each time the yacht gave a heavy lurch the navigator was thrown against the deck-beams overhead. Fortunately this difficulty had been experienced in the practice gale before the race, so before the start sheets of sorbo rubber had been secured to pad every projection, besides the whole deckhead immediately above my head when plotting. This saved many a bruise, but an unforeseen effect gradually came about: the sorbo soon became saturated with water, so as I was thrown up to hit it a squelch of water spurted down to add to the dampness.

Life at that time was not comfortable. Each sail-shift through the night left me soaked as I worked on the foredeck for most of them. Yet after the sail-shift came the navigator's task of plotting each change of course, and logging each shift; to do that in wet clothing would make the chart and log-book a soggy mush, so at first I stripped off my oilskin top and changed my wet shift and jersey after each sail-shift. By the morning every polythene bag full of dry clothes in my locker had been used, while the plotting chart and the log-book were getting damper and damper. A godsend then was a special waterproof chart produced by the U.S. hydrographic department specially for this race; it was said to stand up even to spilt Martini cocktails without being harmed, but by the time it had become the plotting chart in *Belmore* the conditions were hardly suited to cocktails; yet it had a new use as umbrella, protecting navigational books and at times the navigator's head as well from the spray that aimed for the chart-table.

I also had a headache. This was understandable when I saw the hole in the cockpit-locker lid made by the boom end after bouncing off my head; however, the damp and trying conditions below, following a night without sleep, were in themselves a breeding ground for headaches, so I was not alone in this slight hindrance to renewed effort.

But there was never a moment's doubt in my mind that this was the critical time of the race. The gale I had prayed for had arrived, and *Belmore* had come through it very well; perhaps, I thought as the yacht plunged, it might have been possible to keep the mainsail on her, as the wind was moderating when it was lowered. Yet we still had all our sails undamaged, and she had lost very little; we could not know then that three other yachts were dismasted, two had lost their rudders, six men had been washed overboard, and numerous sails blown out; but I knew that our gear was intact and we had passed many yachts in the night. The vital point to decide was when to hoist mainsail and force on with full 'boost-pressure'. This was more a matter of crew ability than anything else; the conditions were rough enough for a human error to set us right back, apart from danger to my crew.

I realized already that I had squandered crew effort during the gale, particularly by increasing sail around midnight when I followed too closely on a temporary easing of the wind. This had meant four extra sail-shifts without gaining any appreciable distance over where we might have been had the reefs and the working jib remained through a few minutes of more moderate wind. We had made eighteen sail-shifts in the gale, and that had used up a great deal of energy; to change up to mainsail prematurely would be a setback to the morale of exhausted men, but the change up at the right moment, with conditions improving, might allow the crew to take full boost for the last seventy or eighty miles of the race.

It was just before 9 a.m., Eastern Standard Time, that I judged the moment had come. I warned that all hands would be needed in oilskins shortly, but myself decided to wear shorts and a football shirt only, as all my clothes were soaked. There were no other yachts in sight, and I was not at all certain of our position, but that would clarify as the weather improved.

It was to be flat out to the finish.

We had a first-rate sail-shift from trysail to mainsail; she was bare abaft the mast for little more than a minute, and settled down under seven rolls at precisely the same speed as she had been making under the trysail; she had logged 17·6 miles in the previous three hours, and the speed under mainsail showed as a fraction under six knots. *Belmore* was very well heeled, and I could walk easily up the sloped mast with the ciné-camera in a polythene bag to take a picture from above the spray level.

An hour later the wind freed a point; with sheets slightly eased we began the steady increase of sail to keep her sailing at her fastest; first a bigger genoa, then two rolls shaken out in the mainsail; two more rolls out; then sights had established a position line, so we altered course five degrees which brought the wind a trifle further ahead. The run for the afternoon watch was 29·6 knots, and around seven and a half knots is exciting enough in a yacht 26·5 feet on the waterline.

The sun was shining between occasional clouds as George came up to take over the dog watches at 4 p.m.; the sea was moderate with no more pounding, wind-force five to six, and working jib-sheets just eased. This was the time that made those middle-watch trials seem worth while; the radio from Bermuda told us that no yacht had yet crossed the line, but the first two or three were in sight to the north of Bermuda; we had only about sixty miles to sail and the scratch boat had to give us twenty-five hours of handicap.

Belmore herself seemed to feel the thrill of intense urgency; she hurtled over the waves, swerving to avoid a steep face and cutting disdainfully through any small one. Now she was glorying in it, when a few hours earlier she had been shivering and sometimes stopped as though shocked by too violent a jolt. She was certain of herself, and her motion had a rhythm of confident power.

'Will she take the R.O.R.C. genoa, George?' I asked.

'Not yet, sir. I don't see that she could go faster than this.'

Soon afterwards a noise like a gun-crash above the chart-table almost catapulted me out of the hatch and straight to the halyards at the mast. The weather-runner had let go, and the mast might be going with it. George also acted instinctively and threw over the tiller to bring her about.

We had practised this failure several times; the standard drill was to leave the foresheet set up so that the yacht would come round hove-to with the foresail backed. However, as she came about I saw that the fittings were still intact, and the failure was in the shackle that joined the runner to its tail-pendant, which passed through blocks to the runner lever. Mike had also shot up on deck almost instinctively with his repair bag, so we would quickly be in action again, and I decided it would be best not to kill her speed, even if it was taking us momentarily away from our destination.

I ordered the second hand of the watch to check the weather foresheet; but habit is strong, and he did not seem to understand. I roared, and he let it go reluctantly, obviously feeling that the skipper did not know the drill. It was perhaps drill that saved our mast on that occasion; by the time anyone had thought out the logical action to take when the runner backstay lets go in such a wind, the chances are that the strain of butting into the next wave would have proved too much for the light standing-backstay. But habit can also be a tyrant and drill well taught cannot be modified in a hurry without something stronger than its tie.

It was less than two minutes before *Belmore* was back on her course, still rampaging through the water. It proved her fastest hour of the whole race with a logged run of 7·6 miles. A couple of hours later we were under full mainsail and the C.C.A. jib, while the wind had lost a couple of figures on the Beaufort scale. Soon after the runner failure we heard radio news that *Venturer* was across the line at St. David's Head; she was a very large yawl of seventy-two feet overall length, and as she started an hour before us we had well over a day for the forty-five miles to beat her on handicap.

Things seemed better than ever; *Belmore* was still sailing at near seven knots; sunshine and aspirins had dispelled my headache, although there was an infernally tender spot on my head. There were no yachts in sight. I was quite certain that we had overtaken some fifty yachts in the gale and fairly confident that few crews would have been quicker than mine to get their yachts going at their best after the blow. I was even willing to forget about *Finisterre*.

The sun was low before we sighted another yacht. Then three or four appeared, all pointing well to windward of

15 The sloop *Doncherry* of Class E dismasted in the Bermuda-race gale

16 *Belmore* finishing the Bermuda race to take second place on corrected time out of 135 starters

Belmore. 'Let them,' I said. 'I am sure we are going straight for the buoy.' One was *Anitra*, overall winner of the last Fastnet race, and high up in the rating of Class C; another appeared to be *Enchantra* of Class A, while a third was identified as *Petrel*, the second-highest-rated yacht of the whole fleet.

'I hope your navigation is right, Skipper,' queried Tim Sex.

'I hope so too. Perhaps they are allowing a couple of miles in case the wind heads us. I'm going straight for the mark; those ones won't worry us, but *Finisterre* may be ahead there and we must take a risk to beat her.'

And that is just where *Finisterre* was at that moment; she was eight miles nearer the first turning mark than *Belmore*, and a trifle further to leeward; had the wind headed us we would not have lost position relative to her.

Dusk came, and the loom of Gibbs Hill Light appeared just as the calculations for two of my four star-sights were plotted. We were three miles ahead of dead reckoning; north-east buoy was right on the bow. Slowly the fresh breeze eased as we came up on the land, and no aspirins could stop my headache then. I felt that only the finishing-line could do that.

Close to the north-east buoy, ten miles to go, we rounded up, nearly hard on the wind; *Anitra* swept by, and *Rhubarb* of our own class was right in our wake; she was the first E-class yacht we had identified that day, but she had to give us seventy-five minutes.

George kept a close ear on the radio broadcasts. A score of yachts from Classes A and B were home, then came *Cyane* to lead in Class C, but I reckoned we should have many hours in hand from any of them.

'No mention of *Finisterre*?' I asked for the umpteenth time, knowing that she gave us 50 minutes 54·3 seconds. 'We should be there in about an hour.'

'This *Belmore*-time is a bit of a snag now, as they are broadcast in Bermuda-time,' said George, 'but I think we are

G

getting reports about an hour after they finish. We are not home and dry yet.'

Then came the next buoy. Five miles to go in a light-wind beat with a nasty little swell that knocked her speed down. We were holding *Rhubarb*, but only just, while a yacht astern of her was catching us steadily. The yacht ahead tacked and we saw she was *Pipe Dream* in our class; but she gave us an hour and a half handicap.

It was the longest five miles at the tiller I can remember for ages, and conditions were thoroughly difficult for steering. George had left the radio and gone forward to tell the genoa for me.

'You're pinching her, sir,' he warned, after a half-dozen hails of 'Lifting'.

Slowly, so slowly, we came up to the bows of H.M.S. *Ulster*, anchored at the seawards end of the line. The yachts ahead rounded her and returned in our direction; *Viking* we saw going inshore with another yacht, then *Anitra*.

'No signs of *Finisterre*?' I queried.

'No,' came the general reply. But we had not identified the yawl going in with *Viking* towards St. George's Harbour.

Motor-launches came up close and flash-bulbs glared, but we had seen that happen to each yacht ahead; there was a cheer from their crew, but that too might have happened to each one.

Still a cable's length ahead of *Rhubarb*, we were over.

'Take this ruddy tiller, George,' I said. 'I'm too tired to do a thing. Go where you like; I'm going below.'

Barry was down the hatch before me. 'This is what you need, sir,' as he handed me a glass.

Through the hatch I heard a hail from the H.M.S. *Ulster*; it was the voice of David Hallifax, her second-in-command, who had assisted with the planning of our venture and navigated *Belmore* in her last Bermuda race.

'*Finisterre* beat you by twenty-five minutes according to my calculations,' he shouted, coming sharply to the point.

'What about the others?' shouted George from the tiller.

'There aren't any others,' came the reply across the water. 'You are second—in the fleet of course.'

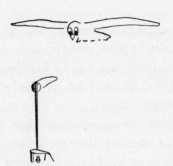

8

Doubts and Conjectures

BELMORE was second on corrected time in the whole fleet of 135 ocean-racers. Twenty-five minutes and twenty-five seconds behind *Finisterre*, this was the first time that any yacht foreign to the United States of America had come within one hour of the Bermuda Trophy.

Her achievement was encouraging when considered without any account of handicap allowance. She had beaten, boat for boat, a hundred yachts larger than herself; this included every one of the yachts in Class D, all but four in Class C, more than half of Class B, and seven of Class A.

Although it was a slow race, *Belmore* had averaged exactly five knots over the course. During nearly half the time the wind had been abaft the beam, and just over a quarter of the time she was sailing close-hauled; she had started hard on the wind in a light breeze, encountered a gale from ahead, covered a hundred miles broad-reaching at near her maximum speed and finished again beating to windward in a light breeze. There had been something of everything.

To beat a hundred bigger yachts she must have been a fast and able boat, well equipped for the whole range of ocean-racing conditions. But there was a great number of other fast, able yachts, with equipment at least as complete. The course she had taken was no different from that steered by many other yachts, although she had certainly gained as much help from the Gulf Stream meander as any other competitor, and more than quite a few.

Her success then, relative to the many good yachts that she beat, was surely an indication of crew ability; the perfect crew performance can only come from such intense concentration and long experience, that no ocean-racing crew is ever likely to reach it; in every watch and every hour there was scope for improvement on board *Belmore*. Yet over the whole period of five and a half days the crew rated high in their ability to keep their yacht going near her best performance; this had been the whole object of the careful sail drills and comprehensive discipline; the habit of discipline gives the skipper a firm grip on the reins to control crew effort, which is especially valuable when this control needs to go against human instincts. Thus it is natural to be excited and enthusiastic at the start, draining energy by emotion when perhaps it is best stored for the occasions when 'boost-pressure' is needed. It is natural to make more effort in daylight and relax the pressure at night; a growing gale may exhaust a crew when their efforts may make little difference to her speed, and thus leave too small a reserve for the race-winning period that comes as the gale moderates.

'What bad luck!' exclaimed all those we met at the finish, 'to be beaten for first place by only twenty-five minutes.'

The truth was that fortune had favoured us quite amazingly. The fog at the start, the unusual Gulf Stream meander, the long periods of light spinnaker work by night and the gale near the end, were all just what was needed by the crew of *Belmore* to enable them to make use of the training they had endured or enjoyed.

Nor at the time did I feel the slightest disappointment that we had not beaten *Finisterre*, when the margin was so narrow. My feeling at first was that our performance in *Belmore* exceeded what I had expected, considering the need to re-organize the crew just before the start; twenty-five minutes represented the superiority of the crew of *Finisterre* on that particular race, with its full range of ocean-racing trials. Carleton Mitchell assured me that not a thing had gone wrong in *Finisterre*'s race, and she had performed with particular success during the gale.

Finisterre is obviously an able and well-equipped yacht to win the Bermuda race three times. Yet in that race there were many other yachts similar to her and created by the same designer, whose yachts incidentally won first place in each of the five Bermuda-race classes. I had no doubt at all that her success over these others came from the experience of her crew, and the exceptionally able leadership of her skipper. To get within twenty-five minutes on handicap of such a crew is not bad luck in suffering a narrow defeat; it needed almost a miracle of good luck to have got so far.

I was very pleased with the result, but very exhausted from the protracted effort. It was a Friday by the time we secured in St. George's Harbour, and there was little enough time before the start of the Transatlantic race the following Thursday. The general plan was to clear up and relax for the next three days, and then use three days in intensive preparations for the next race. I badly needed a real rest myself, and six men is a crowd in harbour, so I decided to hand the yacht over to George and suggested that he take her round to Hamilton when convenient, arranging a berth that suited him best; I hoped that the crew would get away from the yacht as much as possible, with washing of clothes to be done, besides any personal matters to be completed that had been shelved during the hard work of training, and the Bermuda race itself.

It is sometimes quite difficult to re-establish the habit of several consecutive hours of sleep, so quite shamelessly I took a couple of sleeping-pills to ensure good rest and woke feeling none the worse from them. It was intriguing to hear the adventures of our competitors, and each day came new tales of hazards in the gale. The news of the race reached England, announcing the victory of *Fininsterre* and apologetically the papers added that the best British yacht was thirty-fifth; this was true in that *Belmore* was thirty-fifth to cross the finishing line, but it took no account of the different times at which each class started, nor of the handicap allowances; by the same criterion *Finisterre* should have been called thirty-first. However, in America the news seems to have been reported in a way more easily understood, as our first cables of congratulation came from there. A day later full reports seem to have been published in some English papers, and we were delighted to get many messages from friends and supporters; the first came from Tommy Steele, *Belmore*'s owner, and next from John Illingworth, who had skippered her into third place in the Bermuda race two years before.

The third evening I met one of the crew, rather unsteady on his feet.

'Still celebrating?' I suggested.

'No, sir, drowning sorrows.'

'What on earth has happened?' I asked.

'Well, we've failed, sir; that's all about it.'

'Of course we were told to win,' I said, 'but second place is the best a British yacht has ever done. That's no failure. Look at all those cables from clubs and people.'

'They're just your friends, sir, and that's all. There's not been a word from the set-up we've been racing for. No comment means they don't think much of it; all that ruddy sweating was just a ruddy waste of time.'

'Rubbish! I represent our organization out here, and I've told you how ruddy well you all did.'

'Well I think they might take some notice.'

'They took enough notice to get Barry out to America in a rush when I cabled for him,' I protested; 'and that's the sort of support I need. There's the Atlantic race to come and if we win that there will be all the applause anyone can want. We've got to do that first.'

'And pump all the way over, I suppose, while jelly-fish swim in through the seams.'

Perhaps we had not done so well after all, and I began to think back over that gale. Should we have sailed her a good deal harder than we did?

Certainly no sails had carried away, and the water she took in never came anywhere near the limit of the pumps; it was fear of collision that first made me take the mainsail off; it was fear of damaging the hull that delayed hoisting the trysail; and it was saving of crew energy that dictated the time when the mainsail was set. Should I have taken more risks and driven the crew the harder? Looking back we never got within two boat-lengths of hitting another yacht during the gale; the hull could have taken more, and the crew finished the race with ample strength left, even if I was almost exhausted myself.

So it was logical to agree that she could have been driven harder; but that can probably be said of almost every yacht in every race that is not driven to the point of disablement. How could we have done better in *Belmore*? In each point where harder driving would have been possible the decision came back to the skipper. My judgement was probably more cautious than events showed to be essential; the reason for this was partly a matter of my organization, which left too much to the skipper when acting as navigator as well. Going forward to assist sail-shifts in the first part of the gale was a mistake; it was splendid fun, but a Bermuda-winning crew needs to be beyond the stage where the skipper puts on pressure by throwing himself at the genoa to cut seconds. He should, perfectly, do less than anyone else, and reserve his energy for making the right judgement when everyone else is tired. In a gale the crew are hammered about like a boxer taking on a man two weights above his class; they are battered and punch-drunk after a watch on deck; the skipper should be fresh enough to take a more balanced view when conditions are changing. When wet, bruised, exhausted, and banged on the head, judgement may well be at fault.

That is the whole game of ocean racing; the man who could organize his crew perfectly, inspire them to exceptional effort, and then judge situations faultlessly, might well have won that Bermuda race even against Carleton Mitchell in *Finisterre*. To be a better man at the game than Mitch is a high standard.

Conjecture should not be content with limited situations. 'If only we had done so and so' should be tested against the side-effects. It is possible to argue that it was yet another stroke of excellent luck that *Belmore*, which was driven harder than 133 other yachts, was not driven even harder still; when the gale had moderated her weather runner let go, but no damage was caused and little delay resulted; the failure was due to a tested shackle fracturing under a heavy load, and had she been driven harder it is reasonable to assume that this rigging failure might have happened the sooner. If it came about when the sea was as rough as it had been a few hours earlier it is quite likely that she would have been another of those yachts that lost their masts in the race.

But the doubts had crept into my mind. Had I really driven her as hard as the yacht and her crew training would have allowed? With these doubts came tinges of disappointment.

It was Carelton Mitchell himself who did most to allay disappointment. 'We had a superb race in *Finisterre*,' he said. 'But I was never on the outside of a force eight round-up before, and hope I'll never be again.' Once more I was content that to come within twenty-five minutes of *Finisterre* under such conditions was no failure. Next day came the cable, somehow delayed in delivery, to show that our club was well satisfied as well.

The intense training and all-embracing effort of a really hard-sailed Bermuda race takes a great deal more out of men than they realize at the time. When, after that, they are faced with a very long voyage in a small yacht, it is a severe strain on their nerves; only Mike among my crew had ever before sailed a race anywhere near as long as the 600 miles of the Bermuda race; and none had been able to imagine beforehand what it meant to be driven by that urgency which was essential if we were to keep among such yachts as *Finisterre*, with a far more experienced crew.

Many times had I told them beforehand that the Bermuda race conditions would be moderate compared with the certainty of gales in the Transatlantic race. The prospect of a race six times as long, and meeting weather very much more severe, was enough to cause some concern to those whose experience in small sailing craft was rather limited. In my previous Transatlantic races, which each followed closely after much easier Bermuda races, I had seen among rivals the nerves of experienced yachtsmen become jagged in the period before the start; this time we were not racing straight to the English Channel but into the far more tempestuous waters approaching the north of Scotland. I knew, too, of cases where the resolve to win had collapsed temporarily onboard small yachts in mid-ocean races.

My whole scheme of preparation for the Transatlantic race, from the time any man was accepted as a member of the crew, was aimed at keeping the yacht sailing hard throughout the long days and nights of the Transatlantic race; the test would be the gales in mid-ocean, and the ability to keep sailing hard through night after night of hard cold weather. To my mind this required a steady indoctrination into a discipline far more rigid than any that would be ample for less severe tests; to win it needed the discipline of Scott's journey to the South Pole, or of a submarine setting out on a wartime patrol in enemy waters.

Such discipline had been part of the plan; it included a deliberate break immediately after the Bermuda race, and I had urged each man to spend at least a night or so away from the environment of the yacht, and freed of the restraint of our yacht habits. I knew it would need some pressure to enforce this break, as the habit of self-discipline is not easily broken and each man felt the responsibility for his department deeply. I knew, too, that relaxing the spell of tight discipline would help to resolve some of the anxieties that chased round the subconscious minds of those strained by severe trial. Alcohol is a valuable help in easing nervous tension in some, and I took care to see that each of the crew had a private chance to let fly their feelings to me if emotional pressure needed some safety-valve.

Again that had been the plan from past experience, but a weakness in this was that although an outburst of hidden anxieties is a relief to the teller, it may put an extra burden on the recipient.

I was feeling fit after two or three days of rest, relieved of all day-to-day details in the yacht; but my confidence was shaken on hearing some unhibited feelings let loose. Never did I doubt that we could make a safe passage across the Atlantic, but I began to doubt seriously whether we would be able to keep up, in the western ocean gales, that pressure of human effort that I felt necessary to beat bigger yachts.

Belmore had a possible leak, and I remembered the effect ten years before when *Samuel Pepys* was leaking badly in a Bermuda race; we could not find the source of the leak for some time, and the setback to hard racing was far greater than the mere effort of pumping for twenty minutes in every half-hour; when at last Donald Flux had found the cause of the trouble in an ill-fitted hull valve under the cockpit, the relief was like setting the repaired spinnaker again after the last remaining one had been rent by a squall. The hull of *Belmore*, which we thought was leaking in the Bermuda-race gale, now became a source of worry; it was made no better by one of the crew diving under the yacht in a snort mask and coming up to say that the seams had opened up under the mast. It was impractical to get the yacht out of the water in time for the start of the long race as already there was a queue of far worse damaged yachts waiting for the slender slipping resources of Bermuda before they could sail back to America.

I got hold of Mike and we made a careful inspection together. He was a fully trained engineer with ample knowledge of boat construction, besides sound experience of his own ability in making good repairs; so it was reasonable to ask the specific question whether he considered her fit for a Transatlantic race without examination out of the water.

'Absolutely fit, sir,' he answered. 'If there is any loose caulking, and it does come out with further pounding, I can promise to make a repair under way. She's completely sound.'

My doubts about racing her hard shrunk to a mere trickle. I was confident again that not only would Mike cope if the bottom fell out of the yacht or the mast fell over the side, but also that somehow we would keep her racing however tough the weather.

Such extreme efforts so close together as these two races can easily use up more nervous energy than the crew can generate themselves. They can borrow from others, and every bit of encouragement adds to this store of energy.

Rest from nervous tension also needs outside help when time is so short. Probably only a woman has the patience to make the perfect listener that allows a man to dispel his uncertain worries of the unknown, and at the same time to reassure him that his efforts are worth while. Probably few of the tough crew-men among our rivals would be prepared to allow any credit for their he-man achievements at sea to their ladies, who had flown down to Bermuda and acted as psy-

chologists, sympathizers, and diplomats to all those in their
husbands' yachts. Yet I know quite well that when three weeks
later it was touch-and-go whether my crew could endure
another night of driving into a gale, the help we had received
from friends was one of the factors that kept these tough seamen going. Some of the passengers we had met in the *Ebro*
lived in Bermuda and had offered assistance as soon as we
returned to the island. Mr. and Mrs. Robins met us at St.
George's Harbour and straight away took off two soaked men
and half a dozen sail-bags packed with salt-sticky clothes; it
was just the start of a week in which she sorted clothes and
nerves in that delightful feminine way that makes men think
it is all their own work. Well may seamen drink to the health
of the ladies.

9

Atlantic Race Adjustments

IT WAS three days to clear up and let down our hairs from
the emotional pressure of the Bermuda race; then three days
to prepare for the race to Sweden. Fortunately *Belmore* had
suffered no damage to sails beyond the repair by a few
stitches, and no rope had parted. But the yacht had to be
provisioned for over a month at sea, and every item of her
equipment checked and re-stowed. This could best be done
in some quiet corner alongside a wharf, but there were rival
needs that could more easily be satisfied if we stayed at the
berth beside the Royal Bermuda Yacht Club. The result had
to be the compromise of reducing the time in each position
which was thwarting for each man whose job could have
been done better in the other berth.

At last a time and date was published for a meeting of
skippers in the Transatlantic race, at which we would be given
our instructions, learn who our class opponents would be, and
the amount of our handicap allowances. Only then did we
know the number of yachts in the race; three hopeful starters
had been turned down by the committee. That left seventeen
for the course to Sweden; one more would watch the start
and then cruise along the course to the same destination.

Belmore was put in Class C, competing against three other
yachts of similar size. Highest in the rating list of this class was
Yngve Cassell's Swedish cutter *Casella*, which the previous
year had won the King's Cup for best of all classes in the

premier long-distance race of Scandinavian waters; she was a Koster-type yacht, 28·7 feet on the waterline, but her overall length was five feet shorter than *Belmore*, to whom she had to give over eleven hours in handicap. Next came the jib-headed yawl *Delight*, a near relative but slightly enlarged version of *Finisterre*, sailed by a crew of eight of which Wright Britton, from the Massachusetts Institute of Technology, was the skipper; *Delight* gave us in *Belmore* a handicap of five hours and twenty-six minutes for the 3500-mile race, and as she had placed fifth in the fleet for the Bermuda race we looked on her as our special rival. Lowest rating of all was *Danegeld*, to whom we had to give four hours and fifty minutes in handicap.

. At the conference the position of drifting icebergs right in our direct track was given, so yachts were ordered to pass outside a position 'A', which would give a clear berth from the ice. Then we had to pass north of the Isles of Orkney, but otherwise could go where we liked to get from Bermuda to the Skaw lightship, off the tip of Denmark.

It was interesting to look at the faces of those gathered in the committee room of the Royal Bermuda Yacht Club. They were Americans, Swedish, German, and English; all were men of influence and strong personalities, but it was hard to find any other common feature that identified them as skippers of among the hardest-sailed ocean-racing yachts in the world. Presided over by Jerry Trimmingham of Bermuda, representing the Transatlantic-race sailing committee, the discussion was entirely technical, until Henry Du Pont, chief of the vast Du Pont empire and winner in Class C of the Bermuda race, put in a strong plea for sound seamanship by carefully observing proper safety precautions. It was the right thing that one of the senior commodores should give this warning, but it was all rather like the final briefing before a tough convoy operation in war, with Hank Du Pont's appeal like the old warning to experienced Masters to be careful, as there were many more battles to come, and no rescue ships available for that particular operation.

The conference was given a kick towards lighter thoughts by Bobbie Lowein, speaking as a foreign competitor to this American-Swedish-Bermudan-organized race, and as a flag officer of one of England's most hospitable yacht clubs. We were grateful, he explained on behalf of us all, for the splendid organization and hard work of the committee; and the race would be splendid sport, which each would remember for the rest of our lives.

Only with the full race instructions and details of competitors was it possible to assess how we stood, and to complete a strategic plan. By that time I had been onboard every yacht competing against us, and had met most of the skippers several times. Class B of six medium-sized yachts seemed the strongest; I wrote in an article published shortly before the start that this class was an exhibition of the superb, and went on:

Such is their design, equipment and crew that I feel any one of the six B-class yachts is a possible winner of the King of Sweden's trophy for the best corrected time of the fleet; in any company less brilliant it would be reasonable to call each one of them a probable winner. It seems hard to believe that this can be a small boat race.

On her record and skipper *Carina* seemed the most likely winner and dangerous rival; Dick Nye had already won two Transatlantic races, a Bermuda race, and two Fastnets. In the Bermuda race just finished *Carina* was third to *Palawan* in Class B, yet she was only fifty-four seconds behind the second yacht. However, to Dick Nye and the crews of the larger yachts the smaller yachts seemed a major menace to their hopes; *Carina* had to give two days and six hours in handicap

17 *Belmore* sailing off Bermuda under her second (R.O.R.C.) genoa

18 *Belmore* sailing out to the start of the Transatlantic race with 3500 miles to go

to *Belmore*, and in the Bermuda race just finished, over a course one-sixth the length, *Carina* had finished under six hours ahead.

The long-range weather forecast also played a large part in the decision of our overall race strategy; it suggested that for the first 2000-odd miles the general wind would be between south-west and west, averaging fifteen knots, with gusts to twenty-five knots. For the last 1500 miles the forecast gave a 70 per cent probability of winds with an easterly component, that is ahead. The forecast also foretold one or two well-developed pressure cells, while between Newfoundland and Scotland, with mean winds of thirty-five to forty-five knots.

I assessed that during the long run with fresh winds nearly astern, *Belmore* would be at a disadvantage compared with the yawls, which could set mizzen staysails, and particularly be at a disadvantage compared with the larger yachts which would be able to develop maximum speeds in such fresh winds; the small yachts, too, could develop around their maximum speeds, but the square root of *Carina*'s waterline length was some 20 per cent greater than the square root of *Belmore*'s, so with maximum speeds in proportion to these square roots, a run over half the course might take under such conditions twelve days for *Belmore* and ten days for *Carina*, thus giving *Carina* a position greatly ahead of her handicap allowance.

The time when *Belmore* should expect to catch up on this disadvantage would be in variable winds mainly from ahead, but I felt that the real opportunity for *Belmore* would come in the gales that blew with the low-pressure cells; the pilot chart of the North Atlantic showed south of Iceland a square on our course with a gale frequency for that month of 6 per cent. It was there that I felt our main advantage lay, as in proportion to her sail area a small yacht has a stronger crew than the large ones; she should therefore be better able to keep set the sail area that gave the maximum speed in the changing conditions

H

of a gale. I felt that another good time for *Belmore* would come on the approaches to northern Scotland, partly due to my familiarity with those waters, and partly from my confidence in the ability of our navigational equipment for making a racing landfall in rough conditions.

So the strategy evolved was to keep close to the Great Circle on a 1150-mile leg to Point 'A', off the banks of Newfoundland; then another Great Circle for 1500 miles to Rockall banks; after that it was just under 400 miles over the North Scottish banks to Orkney, and finally 400 miles across the Atlantic Sea to the Skaw. As far as Rockall, the Great Circle route would be the guide, with no attempt at finding better currents or weather conditions elsewhere.

We would race quietly in the fresh following winds and build up a reserve of strength ready to put on pressure during gales or calms. The larger yachts, if sailing well, would soon be far enough ahead to get in different weather from us, so it would be guesswork how they were faring, unlike in the Bermuda race when no yacht was ever more than fifty miles ahead of us. Thus our racing strategy was aimed at winning Class C, and would trust that this would stand up to the rest of the fleet.

In my last race across the Atlantic, on the course from Bermuda to Plymouth, my strategy had been quite different. Then the aim had been the largest yacht, *Caribbee*. That time I assumed that her skipper, Carleton Mitchell, would risk a detour far north of the Great Circle hoping for harder weather, and it was my plan to cover him on the same route and ignore the other yachts that might stick to the Great Circle. But in the race with *Belmore* I was equally confident that on this different course the most likely winners in Class B would stick as closely as they could to the Great Circle, as the racing performances of several were so similar.

I assumed that *Danegeld*, which so far that season had not

been able to hold her own with *Belmore*, would risk some
course other than the Great Circle, in the hope of finding
better conditions; and it was possible that *Casella* might do
the same. But *Delight* had the advantages of the yawl rig when
running, and her performance had been within striking
distance of *Belmore* in the Bermuda race, so I assumed she too
would follow the Great Circle. So the race rival for *Belmore*
would be *Delight*; it was unlikely that we would be in sight of
her for more than a day at the start, but I would keep a plot
of her expected position on the conditions we experienced day
by day.

On the day following the meeting of skippers, Bobbie
Lowein and I came down to the harbour together from
Government House, where we had been staying together as
guests of His Excellency the Governor and Lady Gascoigne.
General Gascoigne was the first Governor of Bermuda to have
sailed in the classic ocean race, and was certainly the first one
to be onboard a yacht dismasted on the course; he was keenly
interested in our much longer Transatlantic race and had
visited each competing yacht. Together Bobbie and I sailed
over in *Belmore* to Ireland Island, where we had planned to
make the final preparations lying alongside together in the old
naval dockyard; neither asked what course the other intended
to take, but we had so frequently discussed the aspects of the
race that we probably both knew fairly accurately what the
other planned.

It was hot work re-stowing all the provisions below, then
packing up unwanted gear for return to England by ship; Tim
patiently recorded the position of every tin, on all of which
he had painted numbers during the passage out from England
in the *Ebro*. He had thirty-one different code numbers for his
tins, a variety of dehydrated soups in polythene packets, stores
of dehydrated vegetables in jars, and vast quantities of bread
stowed in nets above the cabin bunks; these loaves had been

baked a second time when in their packages, and the bread kept so well that we continued to eat it after arrival in Sweden and on until we reached England after five weeks. There was an enormous number of biscuits and Dundee cake, which also kept well without any special trouble. Tim had made advance arrangements to get a supply of new-laid eggs just before we left, but many yachts had these flown in from America, as it was felt that the demands of so many yachts at once would exceed the output of the local hens; ours needed no special care to keep as long as they lasted, but we could have done with a good many more.

Melons, lettuce, cucumbers, oranges, and onions were put on board, and large hands of green bananas intended to ripen after ten days or more. We had no refrigerator so fresh meat could not be taken as the temperature below decks was over ninety degrees in the afternoons.

Mike was responsible for the fresh water and besides fixing a pair of extra water-tanks between the main-cabin lower bunks he had added a large number of plastic jerry-cans and aluminium bottles to carry the amount we needed. This was settled by the racing rules as twenty U.S. gallons per man onboard, which with our crew of six made a total of some 100 imperial gallons to be stowed.

Roy was responsible that we carried enough amps in our batteries. There were no means of charging on board *Belmore* so we carried two large batteries, each with a capacity of 150 ampere-hours, and these were intended primarily for the navigation lights; with the hours of darkness reducing to only two or three when in sixty degrees north, there was ample battery capacity for six weeks of navigation lights conscientiously switched on by night. Domestic use of electricity was small, as the clocks could always be adjusted to bring meals and washing-up into daylight, while the single change of watches in the dark needed only one dim light for the few

minutes of dressing and undressing. It was planned that all
navigation work in the dark would be done by the light of
hand torches, and for these Roy provided a large stock of dry
batteries.

George as mate was responsible for rigging a second life-
line round the yacht, made by securing nylon ropes half-way
up the stanchions to prevent anyone being washed under the
normal single life-line. He also rigged a mast-head rope;
Belmore had no topping lift, and if the main halyard should
part there was no moving rigging to the masthead until this
special line was rove specially for the race.

The navigator's department was again to be handled by
the skipper, so it was for me to check the special folio of
charts arranged for the Transatlantic race, and left in Bermuda
while we had visited America. As in all other departments,
space was limited, so the charts were reduced to those absolutely essential; it was accepted that if the yacht had to abandon
the race and put into Newfoundland, Iceland, Ireland, or
Scotland, we might have to wait for good weather conditions
or seek local help for pilotage; but at least I was familiar with
the most likely coasts, so fewer charts could be carried. For
the sextant there was no spare, and it would be very difficult
to win the race if that fell over the side; so in the Transatlantic
race itself the skipper alone used the sextant; if anyone should
throw our chances over the side by dropping the sextant as
she lurched it would be me.

Inevitably in a boat the size of *Belmore* each department
needed to use some part of the yacht at the same time. To stow
jerry-cans under the cockpit Mike had put ashore the accommodation ladder; Roy had taken up the cabin sole to stow the
batteries below. Yet it was down the hatch, and across the
great hole in the deck, that Tim, assisted by Barry, wanted to
bring a couple of dozen loaves of bread. Through all this con-
gestion the skipper wanted to bring down his charts and

navigational tables, while George could make no more progress on deck until he could get below to the tool locker.

Someone watching, and a small crowd of merchant seamen from ships berthed nearby had gathered around us, must have felt it impossible that the stack of provisions and equipment on the jetty could possibly get onboard; while the conflict of tasks between the departments of the yacht must have made it seem unlikely that the pack of us would sail through the first squall without disaster. Alongside us much the same sort of thing was going on in *Danegeld*.

'We ought to have worked out a drill for this,' suggested Tim, 'and done it all by numbers.'

Yet by late afternoon all was stowed onboard, and crates had been packed for the return of unwanted gear to England; sails were hoisted to set off on the eighteen-mile passage within the reefs of Bermuda for St. George's Harbour. There was some windward work, with the breeze hardening as a dark squall passed close astern; after the parties, the doubts, and the final preparations in sweaty heat that squall was a glorious tonic.

10

The Run to Point Able

THE sun shone modestly past a cloud edge as we jilled around waiting for the start of Class C off St. David's Head, Bermuda. The rain had stopped, the afternoon was cool, and a light breeze blew from the south-east.

We had spent a restful night alongside the dinghy-club wharf at St. George's in company with *Delight*, the 'improved *Finisterre* type' which I had selected as our main rival. Every detail up to the start had been planned so that nothing should arise that could upset the feelings of quiet unruffled confidence that was to be our starting theme. There would be, I hoped, no rush, no hectic sail changes, no intense emotional experiences to drain energy; just a competent start at racing stations, then within five minutes a routine change to watch-running.

To ensure no disturbance from this even tempo I planned to sail from St. George's in very good time, then heave-to near the starting line for an early lunch before the big class went off at noon local time. The mainsail had been hoisted in the rain when a call came from the club window that I was wanted on the telephone.

'Unless it is something to do with this race,' I shouted back, 'please tell the caller to put it through to Sweden.'

Another call from the club window: 'It's vital; perhaps it affects the start.'

Delight, secured inside us, was also waiting to sail as I seized the starting instructions and a pencil before clambering ashore. 'Apparently a last-minute change,' I told George and one of *Delight*'s crew.

'Here is a message from Buckingham Palace,' a voice on the telephone said. ' "To yacht *Belmore*. Many congratulations on your fine performance. Philip." '

I scribbled down each dictated word on the starting instructions with water dripping off my oilskins on to the paper. 'Is there a reply?' asked the telephone.

'All right,' I said, 'will you make to His Royal Highness the message that with humble duty the crew of *Belmore* intends to do better next time.'

'Any change?' asked the crew of *Delight* as I crossed their yacht going back on board *Belmore*.

'Only that we've got to beat you now,' I answered, showing the pencilled message. 'I have cabled back that we intend to win this race.'

'Will the Prince fix the weather for you?' commented a doctor.

'No, but it's the crew that matter,' I answered, 'and this message will fix us. We'll drive on until we drop now.'

We sailed around quietly as the seven great yachts of Class A manœuvred for their start. *Drumbeat* interested us particularly as a British yacht, but most of us knew some of the crews also in each of the four large American yachts: *Dyna*, winner of Class A in the Bermuda race; *Barlovento*, *Ondine*, and the seventy-two-foot overall *Escapade* whose crew came mostly from California. Then some of us had also been on board the two large German yachts: Alfred Krupp's *Germania V*, with her crew of thirteen, and Dr. Kurt Fischer's *Hamburg VI*.

'If I were to run this show,' suggested Mike, 'I'd send off the small class first, and make these great whoppers the grand finale. Us little ones will be a bit of an anticlimax for all those people watching.'

'After the Bermuda race they're scared we might get to Sweden first,' put in Tim rather tersely.

Fifteen minutes later came the six yachts of Class B, racing up together for the starting line as keenly as though it was a twelve-mile course in Long Island Sound.

'There go the pick of the pack,' I said with admiration.

'I'll put my shirt on Dick Nye,' said George.

'All your shirts have holes in them,' retorted Tim. 'Look at *Cyane*; Chick Larkin has joined her from *Finisterre* as navigator, and Hank Du Pont's got most of the same crew that won her class in the Bermuda race; even the newest to the game, Ed Hall, has done three Bermuda races.'

The gun went. Two were just over the line and turned back. 'Those two won't have a hope now,' said Tim. 'Two minutes to re-cross the line is too much in a race only a few thousand miles long.'

'Well, *Figaro*'s got Bobbie Symonette from *Finisterre*, and Knud Reimer's to design them a new bow if they hit an iceberg,' said Mike. 'So Bill Snaith might win this time, even after losing two minutes.'

'They've got to hurry,' added Tim. 'Bobbie Symonette's racing at Gothenburg and then at the Olympics.'

The other one to turn back was *Palawan*.

'Dark horse that *Windrose*,' said Barry. 'Her headstay let go in the Bermuda-race gale, so her place don't mean a thing. She's got some special rating this time by lashing up the centre-board; she'll be all right if there's enough running.'

'Yes, she's got that chap Carlsen on board. You know, the skipper of the *Flying Enterprise* which sank on all the front pages!'

'She's also got Vic Romagna—the chap that trimmed *Columbia*'s spinnaker.'

'Our turn now,' I said. 'Racing stations.'

Probably Class C was rather an anticlimax after these two mighty starts; the onlooker craft moved closer as though gathering in for a friendly bout when the champions had left the ring. The line was ample for each of the four yachts to manœuvre without hindrance from the others; it was all just exactly what I wanted.

Danegeld made a splendid start on the windward end of the line close under the stern of the committee boat; Yngve Cassel, smiling happily, swung his Swedish *Casella* in a gybe under the stern of *Danegeld*; *Delight* was well away at the leeward end of the line and *Belmore* in the centre. With the wind abeam and likely to veer, each end of the line was as good as the other, and so far as we could see all four were within half a boat's length of the line at the start.

'Watch-racing,' I ordered. 'We'll put on the clocks one hour to keep supper in daylight.'

The watch-keeping scheme for this race was complex, so as to give flexibility in varying conditions.

'I can't remember all that,' George had protested. 'Have I got to look up in the log every time to see who is my relief?'

'Yes,' I answered impatiently. 'Unless you ask the cook to read it for you.'

The plan was to divide the day into two sections of twelve hours, each with its separate organization. The stress was given to the night section, lasting from 8.30 p.m. to 8.30 a.m., and in this the crew was divided into two watches of two men, with cook and skipper as extra hands. For the first six hours, from 8.30 p.m. to 2.30 a.m., George was the mate-of-the-watch, assisted by either Roy or Barry, as these two took turns as cook for periods of two or three days. The other night watch was always Mike and Tim, who had together proved such a very strong team in the Bermuda race, and again were called upon for the time that always proved hardest to pile on sail; in practice it turned out that by far the most sail-shifts were made in this six-hour watch.

For the daylight period a lesser degree of readiness was accepted, although in fog or other bad weather it might be necessary to revert to the more tiring two-watch system. From 8.30 a.m. until the evening the watches were of two-hour duration under three mates: George, Mike, and Tim. The second hand of the watch had to be dressed and immediately ready for the deck, but could be below decks if not required; this duty was shared by Roy and Barry, with whoever was cook for the day holding himself ready from after lunch until supper preparations started, and the other one taking the rest. The third man to call was the next mate due on duty; he was not required to be dressed for the deck, but if he should be called out in oilskins he would probably not want to take them off before his own turn of watch came round.

The changes at the half-hour were a concession to feelings. George insisted that to eat breakfast for a month at 7.30 a.m. would be intolerable, but at 8 a.m. would be just reasonable; and similarly with the midday meal and supper. The ship's time can be adjusted by the mere change of the clock's hands, so this human feeling of satisfaction entailed only that the ship's log had to be written at half past instead of the hour; the navigator could easily convert this to the G.M.T. used for his plotting and calculations.

By the time we started half an hour after them the yachts of Class A, going at about five knots, were scarcely visible ahead in spite of the clear day; two or three miles is about as far off as another yacht is visible at sea, except when chance conditions of light show up her sails in contrast to the sky. So we were not likely to sight many rivals in that race after the first day or so. It was a very large yacht, *Constellation*, that remained in sight longest; she was ruled too large to enter the race, but after all those racing had started she set off to cruise along the same course to Sweden. The first evening she made a lovely sight as she closed on our quarter with sails silhouetted against the red sky of the dusk. In the night we overtook her, but next day she passed but remained in sight ahead.

By that time the wind had gone abaft the beam, and our spinnaker was helping to pull *Belmore* quietly through the ocean. Even on the first evening we were grateful for the masthead rope that George had rove; somehow the spinnaker got foul, wound taut round the fore-stay in spite of the phantom jib designed to prevent this. It could be cleared only by going aloft, and neither of the halyards could be used, as one held up the spinnaker and the other the phantom jib, both of which were foul. It would have lost sailing distance to lower the mainsail and use its halyard, so the masthead rope proved its worth when Roy clambered aloft and then came down the fore-stay jumble with its help.

Others may have had troubles with their spinnakers in the light shifting airs with a gentle swell to keep the yachts rolling. On the second night we ran upon a yacht, rolling as though her mainsail was lowered, and with a cluster of lights forward as though the crew had some difficulty.

'Can't make it out,' said Barry from under the binoculars. 'Nearly all the yachts have handling lights, but she's showing nothing aloft. They're shining torches into the sea.'

That was the last we saw of any rival until we reached Sweden.

Before the start Dick Nye suggested that once out of sight of the officials and onlookers we might all lower our sails and for forty-eight hours sleep off the exertions of our six-day stay in Bermuda. Nature clearly did her best; for the first two days there was no wind more than twelve knots, no waves more than three feet high, and no rain or violent squalls. But after that the weather must have felt we needed something to remind us we were racing; the wind increased steadily to a peak of twenty-two knots at noon and then moderated by evening to the fifteen knots which was to be about the normal condition for nearly a week.

This gentle trial showed up a weakness in one spinnaker, whose leech wire parted, then snarled the other spinnaker to show a defect in the phantom-jib drill. Still no rain, so we were sailing fast without the tiresome need for oilskins on deck; even at night it was shorts and jerseys for the watch as they drove her at over seven knots; often the yacht was wave-riding. It was splendid sailing without much real effort.

With running gear tested under such excellent conditions things toughened up; squalls came more often, and usually brought rain and lightning, as well as an increase of wind. The sea increased to as much as six-foot-high waves, with occasionally a swell coming in from another direction. This was ocean sailing, but still in easy conditions, except that during squalls she needed careful steering at near-maximum speed. In broad daylight the spinnaker boom downhaul was carelessly left un-secured so the boom topped up suddenly and wrenched its end fitting to disable the boom.

'That one's had it,' exclaimed Mike with annoyance, after he'd come up to help shift to the second spinnaker pole. There was some belting with a hammer, which I felt was as much to relieve his feelings as to repair the damage, but the spinnaker boom was again declared fit for use.

We were back in the Gulf Stream, steering diagonally across its path. Portuguese Men-o'-War were common and Sargasso weed formed long streaks along the direction of the wind. It was hard to feel at ease running under a spinnaker by night, especially when distant lightning hinted that squalls were around. Each time that the log showed we were getting better speed without the spinnaker it was a relief, and many a night I cursed the first man that thought of using these sails off-shore.

Quite often we increased speed by lowering the spinnaker

and setting a large genoa goose-winged to weather, with another set flying to lee. During one period of twenty-four hours she covered under this rig 183 miles, which bettered any day's running under spinnaker. Perhaps in a brisk sea and fresh wind the spinnaker may not be the best sail for so small a yacht as *Belmore*; certainly it often made her steer like a runaway horse on an icy road, and it was the devil of a job to control the brute if a hard squall came up on us in the dark.

My diary for 4th July recorded:

Headsail rig giving us better speed and noon-to-noon run was 183 miles by sights. This is 7·7 knots and might have some current help as log reads only 160. She's certainly steadier than under a spinnaker, the log line yaws about less and reading is probably better. She is wave-riding up to 9½ knots.

I spent some time taking cine-photos of the waves as she rushed through them; a lovely sight. Perhaps I under-estimated the wind at 15 knots, which is only a high force 4; at any rate it gives us our maximum speed, and I trust is not enough to let the big ones reach theirs. Probably it is, after all. I wonder how *Casella* is faring with her longer waterline length—probably manpower affects her with only four in the crew. In *Belmore* the motion is already tiring, and we've been lucky to get no 'all hands' calls yet.

We should be in pretty good condition now, past harbour tiredness, over normal seasickness (it could return with windward work) and well up in sleep. Of course the bigger yachts would be more comfortable.

Actually on that day *Escapade*, the largest yacht, was 140 miles ahead, which was scarcely enough to hold her handicap compared with *Belmore*; *Delight* was some fifty miles ahead and just where estimated on my plot; this meant that in one-sixth of the race she had already gained nearly enough on us to cover her handicap for the whole race. *Casella* had broken her main boom when its end rolled into the sea at high speed, but she lost little ground while her crew made an excellent repair job as she continued running under a spinnaker.

Other yachts had troubles too. *Palawan* and *Barlovento* both broke spinnaker booms; *Windrose* snapped hers and ruptured the end fittings as well. Many sails blew out in the stiffer squalls; two spinnakers went onboard *Barlovento* and another in *Figaro*; the spinnaker halyard block let go in *Delight* and the head swivel went in *Cyane*. *Drumbeat* was dismasted.

Our worst hazard in that fast thousand-mile run came not from spinnakers but from another ship. The moon had set at the change of the watches at 0230, and an hour later Mike reported a light to port, which at first I thought was another yacht. But it soon showed as a steamer's lights, and the ship turned towards us on a collision course. A mile off we flashed a message 'Please keep clear', but she still came on towards *Belmore*, who was running at seven and a half knots under spinnaker with the wind right aft.

Still the steamer came on.

We could not alter course under her stern without gybing, which in that wind would be a difficult job, so I turned *Belmore* to bring her as close to the wind as she could carry her spinnaker.

Again the steamer turned to close us.

I ordered the spinnaker to be lowered; it took charge, lofted its pole, and fractured the heel fitting. The noise of the spinnaker out of control, and violent motion as the yacht came across the seas, brought the whole crew on deck. No one was very pleased with the steamer, although she had obviously steered over to make certain we were quite all right.

An hour later the wind freshened to thirty knots, and the steamer got blamed for that too.

We were only a few days out when all citrus fruit was finished; grapefruit and oranges were no more, nor were there any melons or fresh salad. Although intended to ripen after ten days or more the bananas were in full flush, and they would soon be over-ripe. It was only then that I realized that all our remaining vegetables, except a few onions, were in tins; even the potatoes were tinned, and we were faced with a long passage ahead with practically no fresh food; this was a thing which I had so often in the past condemned, and in our long races across the Atlantic in *Samuel Pepys* we had never gone without oranges or lemons each day, besides at least one fresh egg per man every day. It was annoying, as I well knew how jaded appetites become without fresh food in the diet; it rubbed in the lesson that I should have checked things more carefully beforehand.

At least we had fresh onions, and ample supplies of vitamin tablets. Personally I developed quite a taste for raw fresh onion, as there was nothing else fresh, and conscientiously I ate a vitamin tablet each day, although its taste could never be satisfying.

Six days out Cape Race was 360 miles away to port. We had been driving very hard for three days on end, and my diary records:

Third day of hard driving and its usual effect on nerves. It is the protracted strain of everything I suppose. . . . My sights were bad, mistakes numerous, and steering not so good. After the moon set, life for a time last night was all rather tedious, the race absurd and 'Oh for home in quiet peace'. The roses must be out and strawberries ripe.

Working dawn sights I thought first we were far south of D.R., then to the west, and next time I re-worked the lot, I just was not certain. Meantime George had insisted in the night that the damaged spinnaker pole was incurable.

The wind eased a bit after breakfast and sea quietened. Shifted to spinnaker to hold our speed. In easy motion again I worked out those four star sights, and all came out right, checked by sun this

19   The yawl *Delight* racing against *Belmore* at the start of the Transatlantic race

20 Eight hundred miles out from Bermuda. Fast running and no oilskins

21 Wave-riding in a steep, lumpy sea

morning; we've done another stupendous 180-mile run and averaged 6.55 for the whole race.

Tension relaxed after lunch and the noon position had been announced. Bedding came up on deck to air, the damaged spinnaker pole was mended by George; those hunted looks of anxiety have gone.

3 days of flat-out running without let up is past. Things not too bad, nearly a quarter of the course sailed and no real set-back; all sails intact, a few ropes need replacement, and both spinnaker poles usable. A tot of whisky in the evening and chicken supper. Light banter; Mike and Tim stand things superbly and they are the youngest; so much for that age theory.

I've decided that from now on every spinnaker shift in fresh condition at night will be an 'all hands job'. The three watch by day routine makes this quite reasonable, and we've had enough mess-ups already.

Next day, 6th July:

In spite of the easing up yesterday, the noon-to-noon run was still 175 miles. Our wind always blows hardest by night.

In the dog watches the air had a different feel, cooler, more velvety, and clearly a change is coming as the wind backed to the south. After dark the wind increased from the south to 23 knots mean speed; steering harder again, and the main boom dragging through the wave-tops; what a terrific pace.

Just after midnight called all hands to get off the spinnaker—quite a fight, but no damage. Set C.C.A. genoa on pole as spinnaker, no loss in speed. Moon appeared fitfully through low driving cloud; sort of time when ashore you'd look up past the trees and say 'No night to be at sea'.

Just before the change of the watch, George said she was no longer fully manageable, and Barry was unhappy on the tiller. Not surprising when she charges off as though all set to broach. Took a couple of rolls in the main; ten minutes later took in two more, and then shifted the C.C.A. for R.O.R.C. genoa; she did 45·2 in that watch.

I

The barometer was falling, and soon after the turn of the watch we ran into heavy frontal rain with a wind veer. Mike and Tim in real racing form; it went 0415—out two rolls in the main; five minutes later, set full main and shift up to R.O.R.C. genoa; at 0500 they came down again to worker jib, and took in a couple of rolls; out again an hour later, and at 0710 set the spinnaker. Being daylight we tried to set spinnaker with three men on deck, but we slipped up and it snarled as the genoa came down; called all hands, and with Roy at the lower spreader we had the spinnaker down in ten minutes. The wind had increased rather suddenly so we set R.O.R.C. genoa on a spinnaker pole, with the worker flying: two rolls on the main. Fifty minutes later Mike had them out. It was another forty-five-mile watch, but by God those two worked for it in rain throughout, and seas upwards of twelve feet from trough to crest! . . . During the passage of the warm front the wind varied from thirty-five knots down to fifteen.

In the forenoon the wind moderated and later the sun's outline showed through the clouds. This was important, as at noon the dead reckoning put us seventeen miles short of Position A, which had to be rounded to port. Again came a glimmer of sun exactly on our beam; from it the sextant angle gave a position-line that passed half a mile outside the point. To be on the safe side with the rules we would run on along that line until five miles past the point by reckoning, or until another sunsight on a new bearing showed we were past.

This point in the middle of the ocean was an occasion to celebrate, so I prepared a small marker buoy from an empty milk tin, and carefully marked on it 'POINT A', with the word *Belmore* on the other side.

The laying of a buoy, even a milk-can type, needs appropriate ceremonial, so at 1535 all hands were called, and a count-down conducted to the exact second when the buoy was to be laid.

'It all looks much like any other bit of sea to me,' suggested Barry.

'Look at that bottle,' shouted George a minute later, pointing at the sea ahead. 'It's ruddy well the sort Dick Nye's whisky comes from. I bet *Carina* laid a marker too.'

11

Western Ocean

Soon after the milk-tin buoy had been laid to mark Point Able, the sun's rim appeared etched on a cloudy background and was deflected to the horizon by my sextant mirror. The sight showed that we had run along the previous bearing line four miles further than necessary before altering course twenty degrees; we had actually passed Point Able at 1450 G.M.T. on 7th July.

'You've thrown away a mile, sir,' said Tim, and quoted back one of my training dictums. 'You'll be sorry if we're beaten by one minute; very sorry.'

Belmore had averaged 6·84 knots for the first leg of 1142 sea miles; it was amazingly good going for that part of the ocean where the more moderate winds might be expected. Our situation seemed splendid, and had we known the actual position of the other yachts, I would have been just as happy. *Danegeld* was 102 miles astern, and had made a detour to the west looking for more help from the Gulf Stream that way; this was what I expected of Bobbie Lowein, as his yacht seemed unable to sail up to her rating; but the gamble had not come off. *Delight*, after a failure of equipment aloft, had lost distance on us during the last twenty-four hours of hard going; she was only twenty miles ahead, compared with the forty I estimated for her on my plot.

My mind was tuned to *Carina*, as the main threat outside

our class, and actually she was then placed best of all some twenty-one hours ahead of *Belmore*; but *Figaro* was the eventual overall winner, and she was then only seventeen hours ahead of *Belmore*. Nearly a third of the course had been sailed, and as *Figaro* had to give us more than fifty-three hours for the whole race, we were holding our own on her with a trifle to spare.

Point Able was more than a pencilled circle on the chart to turn around; it marked a new stage in the course in several ways. It was the point of non-return for the American continent, and from then on if we were damaged, we could not hope to make Newfoundland 400 miles north-westward; it must be Iceland, the British Isles, or the Continent of Europe. From then on there were no more main shipping routes to cross, and probably relatively few ships about until we met trawlers on the Continental Shelf. We were on our own, with nearly 1500 miles of Western Ocean wastes until we came upon the bare pinnacle of Rockall, uninhabited, unlit, and no broader on the waterline than the length of the larger yachts. A lifeboat chart, printed on canvas for use should a ship's crew take to her boats, states of this area 'Winds are often stormy. North-west winds are frequent in winter; south-west in summer.'

In July the main steamer routes from Northern Europe to New York pass through areas where the gale frequency varies between 0 and 1 per cent. At our Point Able, close northwards of these routes, the frequency in July is 1 per cent; from then on along our route it steadily increases to 5 per cent when a thousand miles short of Scotland; then the frequency drops slowly again to less than half that on approaching the Hebrides and Orkney. Five per cent gale frequency, the Admiralty Sailing Directions explain, imply an average of three and a half gale days a month. A gale, for these calculations, meant a fresh gale, force eight or more; it did not include a moderate gale, force seven, with a mean wind speed of twenty-seven to thirty-three knots.

This leg was through an area of Polar Maritime Air, across which depressions and their attendant frontal systems travel regularly. The Western Ocean is traditionally treated with respect by seafaring men; its northern expanses are among the most hazardous of any waters regularly used for ocean navigation.

It was in this wild stretch that I planned that *Belmore* should win the Transatlantic race.

A sample of Western Ocean weather came early. During the first night after passing Point Able, a small depression moved over *Belmore*; for a time it blew briskly, and hurled over the yacht spray that felt cold after our stay in the semi-tropical climate of Bermuda.

It started about dusk, when the spinnaker came down in heavy rain with a gusting south-westerly.

Sea just before dark very rough, grey foam blewn in streaks and cross-waves piled into heaps. Wind 36 knots. Yacht not under control, so considered ordering 'special helmsmen only', but felt this was too unsettling to routine. Steered some time myself and enjoyed it, but feel if I frolic on the tiller I'm wasting my effort which should be saved carefully for any crisis. About ten p.m. lowered mainsail which was torn; Roy repaired split seam in fore cabin. She still ran very fast under R.O.R.C. genoa poled out and worker jib set flying. No sights to work so I did the foredeck work with George at the tiller.

Just before midnight went below to look at mainsail progress. George hollered down that the worker was shy, so went back on deck. At that moment wind veered 7 points to N.N.W., as though someone had switched on the blower from a new direction. Down worker, off pole from R.O.R.C., up mainsail; it was ready just in time to use the same one again. Wind about 20 knots and sea disturbed, but lost its vice with the wind-shift; low cloud cleared, rain stopped, night fairly light with moon behind upper clouds. Got main settled by midnight with two rolls; reaching comfortably at 7 knots, wind abeam, swell astern and new sea only just building abeam. Barometer jerked up.

2 hours later wind down to fifteen knots. Shook out rolls from mainsail, shifted to C.C.A. genny as the watch changed. What with the passing of the cold front, the split mainsail and umpteen shifts, it was still a 40 plus watch to George's credit.

Later that day, 8th July, the wind backed and went light. By breakfast-time the spinnaker was dragging her over the big west-south-west swell which died slowly. I somehow felt we had not got a full share of wind from that blow; the swell had been too big to match the wind; somewhere, not far away, someone might have got wind far stronger than ours.

Sunset made variety from a grey day. As the sun peeped through when nearly down to the horizon, it lit from below the whole trousseau of varied top-cloud; at times in the dusk it looked as though there might be patches of blue overhead, but a shift in the light shewed them to be grey-blue clouds. No star shone through.

Had we known it, 8th July was a grey day in another way. *Figaro*, and the yachts of Class B, began to creep out ahead of us as our wind failed with the passing of our front; in the dog watches *Belmore* scarcely managed three knots. For the day's run to noon on 9th July, we logged 113 miles, even if the current added another twelve; *Figaro* covered 160 miles that day, and we could not afford her thirty-five miles a day.

The next day was another poor one for *Belmore*. Under a leaden sky with a northerly swell, flukey winds gave her a day's run of scarcely over a hundred miles to noon on 10th July; *Windrose*, the nearest of the Class B yachts to us, recorded 185 miles for the same period, *Anitra* sailed 192, and *Figaro* was two days ahead of *Belmore*.

We suspected nothing of this, nor of the arm that had reached out from the main Azores High to form a ridge, cutting off Class C from the yachts ahead (see Fig. 1). *Delight* at the time was forty miles ahead of *Belmore* and must have come near to getting on the right side of the ridge; had she done that *Belmore* would certainly never have won her class, and it might well have been that *Figaro* would not have won the overall race either.

On board *Belmore* we assumed hopefully that whatever light conditions we got, the others would get also. We relished the fact that oilskins were not needed on deck, with no spray flying; Mike shifted some fresh water, emptying one of the large cabin tanks into plastic cans which were empty; in the first ten days nineteen gallons of fresh water had been used, which worked out as only two and three-quarter pints per man per day; however, we had started with a few odd cans of fizzy drinks, and eight cans of beer, so our consumption had been helped out by these.

Tim did his first major food replacement from the bilges, so the galley was again bulging with tins at the tip of the cook's fingers as he worked. Roy got in some sketching when off watch; Barry struggled with crossword puzzles, and I worked out that even with the two very light wind days, our mean daily run for the race was still 155 miles, or 6·46 knots.

At that rate we would finish on 22nd July and *Carina* must get there by 19th to beat us; but there are still 2,100 miles and some gales ahead. I anticipate a third day of quiet, and then a blow again. However, yesterday's hopeful fall in the barometer proved no more than a check in the rise, which now persists.

A tot again this evening; in such light conditions, with the nights light too, hazards are small. But light, flukey winds and little action are tiresome, so I feel the drink is valuable as a strain-reducer. This evening it was to celebrate 'Clear of the ice-line'.

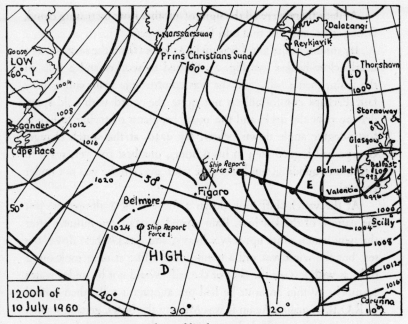

FIG. 1. A ridge of high pressure intervenes

This light weather is certainly trying; yet surely it is as trying for our opponents, and perhaps betters our racing chances if they all get it. It would be hell if some did not.

The next day was as quiet as expected.

Another leaden day of dull maritime polar air. Odd little gusts come down to our level from the different wind higher up. Might just as well be sailing on the upper Thames, with wind slipping through between the houses, as in mid-Atlantic.

No sign of fog since the southern Gulf Stream, in spite of its high probability on the averages up here. Damned lucky, I hate the stuff more than anything. Sea temperature at 60 is just below the air temperature.

This afternoon a wind change to S.S.E. brought down the spinnaker. Barometer shows a welcome fall at last.

At dark there were all the signs of another low; increasing cloud, falling glass, and just that odd feeling one gets.

By midnight the wind was up to 25 knots from the south-east—nearly close-hauled (*see* Fig. 2). Shifted to worker and 2 rolls in the main, then 4 rolls, and she was comfortable again sailing very fast. Perhaps comfortable is not quite the word with cold spray driving over the deck, and the usual problems of trying to live at forty-degree angle down below. By 0230, at the watch change, George had logged 46·4 in his 6 hours, our best run yet; sea 6 to 7 feet, no pounding, but before the sail reduction she was not under control.

At the watch-shift took down 2 more rolls, 8 altogether; just the pattern of the last low. Rain started at 0240, ten minutes after the new watch came up; it was heavy, and quickly beat down the sea, but the wind was still a young gale; Mike at once took out 2 rolls, as with less sea the foot of the sails would not be under water so much. Within an hour he had out another 4 rolls; then shifted to R.O.R.C. genoa. Again it was Mike in the bows, getting soaked every time she washed down; Tim at the mast merely getting sprayed; Barry at sheets, mostly getting abused; and self at tiller mostly getting impatient.

At sunrise the rain became even heavier, and I expected a warm front, as barometer is down 0·4 inch. But wind increased a spot and we took in 2 rolls with a shift back to worker; then suddenly the rain stopped and we got a quiet patch, so whipped up full main and C.C.A. genoa; too soon, as a new breeze came in from a couple of points to southward; so back to R.O.R.C., which she held until George relieved, having missed his breakfast in favour of sleep; but by then Tim wanted to put on the C.C.A. before he went below.

What a treat to have a pair like that on watch; they certainly worked hard for their watch run of 43·8 miles, close-fetching in a nice little blow, with seas building to very rough at dawn. I laced their coffee with rum when they came below—helps to warm up after six hours of sweating and shivering on deck.

Actually the low-pressure centre passed just south of *Belmore*, and winds over forty knots were reported about a

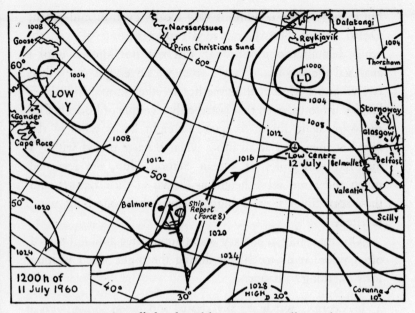

FIG. 2. A well-developed low-pressure cell goes by

hundred miles south of her. However, none of the yachts seem to have done better than her from that blow; *Danegeld* was then two days astern and probably well south of the centre. We about held our own for the day on *Figaro*, and caught up on *Delight*, who was only fourteen miles nearer than us to Rockall at noon.

At that time we reached half-way to the finish, with under a thousand miles to Rockall; our radio gave a good bearing from Ocean Station Vessel C about 150 miles northwards, and that night we picked up the Consol signals of Bushmills well over a thousand miles away.

The blow had been short-lived and by noon we were becalmed, after a couple of hours of light variables that gave *Belmore* less than two knots through a ten-foot-high swell. But the barometer was still dropping and I had hopes of another stir in the night. Why we did not get it is hard to understand, but it shows how conditions vary locally even in mid-ocean; Ocean Station Ship C recorded eighteen knots of westerly wind that afternoon, although this was not known until I analysed the records after the race; we never got more than twelve knots wind at the time her weather should have been handed on to us, even that lasted only a couple of hours before we were again down to seven or eight knots wind in the log. Yet then, and at all times when *Belmore* passed within a hundred odd miles of Ocean Station Ship, she recorded much the same wave height as shown in their reports, and these sometimes seemed bigger waves than our light wind merited.

On 12th July the diary starts soon after midnight, as I often wrote it by torchlight during the night when waiting for something to happen.

In George's watch the sky cleared and moon shone, with a N.N.W. wind quietly getting him along at four point five knots under spinnaker. As soon as Mike and Tim appeared it clouded over and rained again, off and on. At dawn there were ugly cloud banks all round; the biggest had a dark indefinite base, with rising above it dirty white cumulus and cumulo-nimbus clouds; the barometer was dropping again, and they doubted whether the spinnaker would stay up long. However, I felt quite at ease about the weather, in spite of the signs, and as I could get no sights, took a turn at the tiller from Mike, who was very cold. Gave him a tot of rum before I took over; Tim would not have a tot and does not look too well. Those two have had an awful flogging as the tough stuff always seems to chance in their half of the night. No decent wind came; only rain and a shift.

After breakfast we got some sun in spite of the weather threat and low barometer; it was the first time it had got right through the clouds for several days, and was most welcome even if not very warm. We've got much clothing to dry, but as she's on the wind we can't get very far with that. Oh for the stove that Bobbie Lowein had fitted in *Danegeld* for the race.

The continual dampness did not help scratches to heal. I was getting worried about Tim, who looked quite unwell by the end of his morning watch. His arm was worse, although the evening before Mike, as doctor, had tried a hot lint poultice, with another in the morning. The arm was badly swollen, and I began to think what it would be like trying to dress it when the gales came again. Barry also had a swelling on his leg. At midday Tim's arm looked worse again, swollen to nearly twice the size of his good one. A thousand miles from land, no radio transmitter that could be picked up more than fifty miles off; I began to wonder whether I was right to keep on when there was a doctor on board the ocean station vessel only a day's sail back on our quarter. To turn back would be the end of our hopes in the race, and perhaps the swelling would shortly come to a head. I wondered, and Tim himself knew I was wondering; he saw me measuring off the distance on his way to take over his watch.

When Tim came below two hours later, he had made up his mind. 'I'd like to try penicillin, if anyone took in Hans Rozendaal's lesson on how to jab needles.'

It is an accepted thing that if needed, the skipper must give an injection of morphia to any of his crew in real pain. I'd done this before, but did not relish giving injections.

'I'm the doctor,' said Mike. 'Penicillin injections seem the thing—just what Hans told us. I'll do it.'

'I would if I had to,' put in George. 'But I'd need a bottle of whisky first; half for the patient, and half for me.'

The swell was eleven feet high at the time, and the wind was not strong enough to steady her heavy rolling.

'Want to alter course?' I asked Mike as he boiled a kettle for sterilization.

'It'll be all right, sir, as we are. I'm going to go steady, and check every point from the notes before I do it.'

At 2100 the log-book recorded: 'Injected 300,000 units of penicillin in Tim Sex.'

It worked well and by next morning his swelling was under control; but it still needed a good deal of attention until the end of the race. The treatment was entirely approved by a doctor who came on board us after the race, but he doubted whether we need have suffered the various sores, boils, and swellings. I had been annoyed when we ran out of fresh fruit and vegetables so early in the race, but had not connected this with the troubles, as we had ample vitamin tablets on board to make up for the deficiency.

'But how many have you taken yourself?' he asked.

'One a day after the oranges were finished,' I answered; 'and I also had some raw onion most days, as that was the only fresh stuff.'

'Well, perhaps they don't like raw onions, and I doubt if anyone else took those pills judging by the number still left in the bottle,' the doctor suggested. 'Damp conditions and severe strain have something to do with it, but there would have been a better chance of keeping off those troubles with more fresh food in your diet.'

Meantime in mid-Atlantic I was certainly finding our food uninteresting without the fresh fruit and fresh vegetables that we had enjoyed through other Transatlantic races. In the organization I had not paid sufficient attention this time to the food, and my training should have put more zest into cooking, as well as sail-changing.

We were slogging along laboriously through the night, a close-fetch into a northerly wind no more than ten knots. Five knots through the water seems a mere crawl, although just two more knots seems a thrilling rush. Some stars showed in patches before dawn, and I had great hopes with the sextant ready; but once more the clouds covered the sky just before the horizon became visible. Navigation caused me a certain amount of worry, partly from the persistent absence of sun or stars, and partly because we had still not been able to pick up the British time signals, while the continuous W.W.V. American signal was only very occasionally heard on our radio, which could not cope with long-range high-frequency reception. Our deck watch had never recovered since the Bermuda-race gale and had no principles about the time it told. However, the Consol signals came through regularly at night, although after dark the bearings are not too accurate.

The diary read:

It is getting quite cold at night, but the mid-afternoon deck temperature was up to 52 degrees in a rather cool northerly breeze. Birds are frequent, especially fulmers and skuas, but today none of the stormy petrels which had provided a continuous escort since a day or so out of Bermuda.

On 14th July the northerly wind was even lighter, with a high barometer reading; in the evening we were nearly becalmed and George's six-hour watch produced a record low run of 11·2 miles.

We could not guess that *Belmore* was moving to keep in the middle of a 'High' and that the calms did not stretch very far; thus at noon G.M.T., our log showed wind north by west six knots, while at the same time the Ocean Station Ship I ahead reported wind nineteen knots due north, and Station C astern of us reported twenty knots from the south-east. We did not know this until after the race, nor that *Figaro* had in two days covered 347 miles against the run of 262 for *Belmore*. On handicap allowance we could not afford to let her gain more than about eight miles for every hundred we we sailed. *Figaro* was that day far enough ahead of *Belmore* to equal the handicap allowance for the whole race, although we had only sailed 2000 miles. *Delight* was some thirty-five miles closer to Rockall than *Belmore*, but lay well to the northwards; *Danegeld* had caught up and was forty-four hours astern.

Again no star-sights on the evening of 14th July and the diary records:

I am now thoroughly rested, and all the worries have resolved; we've heard the B.B.C. time signals, Tim's arm is greatly improved, and the standard of steering has gone up. Nights are short and the weather has been calm even if dull. So I can feel relaxed and happy about things. Now we really want a good gale, persistent and right on the nose; I'm certain we can take it better than the large yachts which have more canvas to handle per man; we'll be better off than *Casella* and *Danegeld* as we have more crew for the same sail area, while if it's hard windward stuff I'm certain we can catch up *Delight*. Having prayed for this gale, we must be ready to use it fully. George is splendid at steering hour after hour in vile stuff, but it always seems to come out as Mike and Tim that are on watch for piling on the sail as it moderates; that is the key for us. I'll scrap the chance of star sights tomorrow morning and take that watch myself, so that Mike and Tim each get some extra sleep to fatten them up for the job to come. There's been some slogging and slatting in the last few days but now I'm really going to enjoy this race.

12

Storm near Rockall

On FRIDAY, 15th July, the log read at 1030 hours:

Course 075. Log run for hour 7·7 miles. Barometer 29·98 falling. Wind S.S.E. 23 knots. Overcast; heavy rain. R.O.R.C. genoa, 2 rolls in the main.

Rockall was 415 miles ahead; Iceland and Ireland were equi-distant some 550 miles away. This was the area of maximum gale frequency; it was the best time for gales in my race plan. Our whole training had aimed at racing through a really tough gale; it would be fortunate if we could fight it out in the wastes of the North Atlantic with nothing to interfere between the crew and the gale, with no hazards of land and no likelihood of collision. Then it would be the wind and the sea against six men who had drilled for this battle; the game was to win more effectively than the crews of other yachts, unseen nearby.

Just where I had planned as the perfect position, the gale

was coming; it was as though I had won the toss with the weather, and with it the right to select the pitch; but the length of play, and pauses for half-time, would be for the weather to choose.

At the time I had no clue that the last round had gone against me; that the ridge of high pressure which drifted slowly to the eastwards had kept pace with the yachts of Class C, while those ahead were on the downward slope of barometric pressure. That morning the wind was freshening up; it seemed likely to be a daylight gale for *Belmore*, and perhaps partly a night gale for those ahead; for us it would be in the open ocean, while for the leaders there might well be the added worries of land nearby.

As the barometer fell and the wind rose, everything seemed perfect. My crew had been with me, all but one man, for over two months continuously, with some preliminary training before that. They had drilled for this gale through their every action in that time; I knew the strength of each man, and I could assess what he could do best, besides his probable endurance. But it is harder for a man to judge correctly his own limitations.

My excitement increased with the sound of the wind in the rigging; for me the howl of a rising gale is martial music. I had not after all taken the whole of the morning watch, as planned to relieve the strain on Tim and Mike for the coming tussle. During George's watch variable winds before midnight meant several gybes which kept me on deck with the spinnaker set. Then as his watch came to an end at 0230, the signs were clear that a weather change was already in progress a few hours ahead of my expectation; so I took just a couple of hours of that watch to allow Mike and Tim a little more sleep, and then had some myself.

After breakfast I steered for a time. The thrill was exhilarating as she hurtled through the seas at a speed I had never known before, even in that Bermuda-race rush after the gale. It was like galloping an over-fresh horse down a rough slope, with the stirrups lost and the way ahead hidden beneath the curve of the steepening gradient. Riding *Belmore* on a wave face, the tiller was no more effective than tugging at the bit of the runaway horse. 'What would happen now if a rigging shackle let go?' I wondered. She sometimes dashed on, wave-riding uncontrollably for thirty seconds at a time before the wave-crest overtook, and the feel of control came back to the tiller.

At the next sail-shift, 11.05 a.m., I gave George the tiller and hurled myself at the genoa as it thrashed with the easing of its halyard; then up with the worker jib, and two more rolls in the main.

For the sheer fun of it, I went up the mast to the lower spreaders. It was more walking along, than climbing aloft, as the yacht heeled forty-five degrees from the vertical. Standing up there, hugging the mast, the eye was above the wave-tops, and the spray hurtled below my feet with venom, while the rain drove eagerly past my face. It was a magnificent sight of angry seas, although not far off they merged with the lowering clouds and darkening rain. *Belmore*'s bows, plunging in and out of the waves, seemed like the scrum-half as he side-stepped or held on to cut through the mêlée of a fierce rugger game. From that perch above the scrum I could feel detached, and pitied George when a treble salvo of spray hit him one after the other in the cockpit as he steered. 'Blast it.' '—— it.' '——,' I could lip-read the tune and imagine the four-letter words.

No signs of pounding. But when an extra bite in a squall flattened her momentarily, the foot of both foresail and main buried into the water to leeward.

It was time to shift sails again: I must get back to the deck. A tinge of fear, personal, physical fear, brushed my mind. 'Down in all that stuff below?' it said, with its inhibiting suggestion of inaction. 'You can't just hang around here until the mast crumbles,' I told myself, and struck out with dangling legs. Going down from the cross-trees was a good deal harder than getting up.

Soon after lunch we had completed the usual gambit of sail changes right down to spit-fire jib and ten rolls in the main; this left a sail set on the mast very little bigger than the storm trysail. Still the log, hour by hour, showed a speed of over 7·5 knots.

At this time I recorded in the log: 'Gale force 7–8; mean wind speed 36 knots'; probably I was misled by the sea which was no bigger than that for a hearty young gale only two or three hours old; the synoptic chart suggests that *Belmore* should have experienced wind a good deal fiercer at the time. With the four-mille isobars only forty miles apart, in latitude fifty-five degrees, a storm might be expected.

The seaman's storm, force ten or above on the Beaufort scale, means a gale of exceptional severity. If this was indeed a storm, it was only the second I had encountered in a sailing craft after many years of voyaging through every month of the year; my first had been ten years before off Cape Hatteras, a notorious storm area, as was our position 400 miles west of Rockall. Even in thirty years of a naval career, through war and peace, in large ships or small, throughout all the oceans of the world, I had only encountered a handful of storms in the open ocean, although many times I had watched the whole process of a storm from the bridge of a ship that had sought shelter in enclosed waters, or from the exposed shores of an Orkney Island.

In a storm, winds of fifty knots blow at masthead height; the geostrophic wind scale suggests there was a storm where *Belmore* sailed. The weather report, when we received it soon afterwards, told of an intense depression moving slowly; it forecast widespread gales, severe in places.

Feeling that the front must be nearly past us, I went on deck to try a couple of rolls out of the main; it was obviously too soon to give more speed but I wanted to keep up the offensive against the gale, the better to pile on sail if the wind eased in the low centre, or between the fronts if the centre was to the northwards.

Something was going wrong forward as those round the mast struggled to taughten the main halyard, after they had

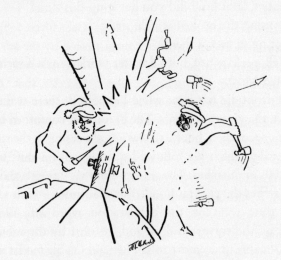

Mike was taking violent steps to do
something

put back those two rolls, following the premature trial of extra mainsail. 'Mike,' I shouted down the hatch, 'I think there's a muck-up on the main halyard winch. Would you have a look?'

Mike joined the group forward, each with his safety-belt hooked somewhere to the rigging, but his was on the long stay to give more freedom of movement. He needed it, and whatever the mechanical failure I could see that Mike was taking violent steps to do something; it was certainly not a micrometer adjustment, as he hurled himself at the job like a prize-fighting blacksmith. 'Luff!' he roared. Then seeing that momentarily I had no control as she wave-rode, he modified it to 'Would you luff, sir, please?'

The job done and the mainsail again taut with its ten rolls, Mike came aft. 'The winch barrel has split right across,' he explained. 'It's quite useless now. Beyond repair.'

'Then we must use one of the other winches, or a tackle,' I suggested. 'But how did you get it up this time?'

'By using the broken winch, sir.'

'Not quite useless then?'

'Well, perhaps not, but I'd better work it myself each time,' suggested Mike.

The front did not clear when I expected; there was no gap between the vigorous fronts. The barometer continued to drop as dusk approached, but there was a slight easing in the strength of the gale, which we followed quickly with a shift to only eight rolls in the main. The sea was then very rough and in the dog watches the cockpit flooded several times.

As time went on the exhilaration wore off. We were bashed by the waves on deck and battered by the movement below, unable to do more to sail her and unable to rest instead. The 'Low' was moving little faster than *Belmore*, and as we were directly in its path we would continue to sail at maximum speed so long as the helmsman, half-drowned in the cockpit, could stick it out. It was one of George's strong points that he seemed able to 'switch off' from even the most intense discomfort, and for hours on end keep alive only those senses that kept him steering a good course. Six hours, I had said at breakfast-time, is the most we are likely to get before the front passes and the wind changes; it turned out to be eighteen hours, and during that time she averaged 7·54 knots. It was eighteen hours with no half-time halt.

Ten minutes before the watch-change at 0230 the rain

stopped suddenly; the barometer had reached the radio-reported bottom of the 'Low', and the whistle in the rigging changed its tune. The sea was very high and lacked control. Once more it seemed that the weather had favoured us inordinately, with each watch-mate getting the conditions in which he shone. 0230 meant Mike and Tim would take over

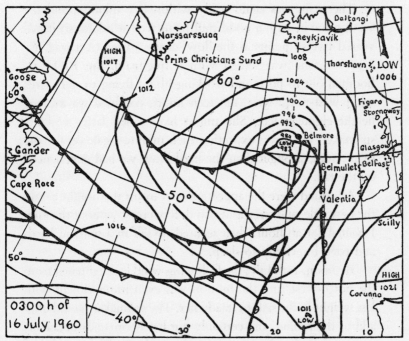

FIG. 3. When the crew matter most
(*Reproduced from an Admiralty synoptic chart*)

the watch; within a few minutes the order to take out four rolls was given.

'Winch managing?' I asked Mike as he came aft to the cockpit.

'Yes, sir, but I hope we don't have to use it too often.'

During that watch it was probably used more than in any previous watch in the race. As the wind eased there was the usual shift, headsail after headsail, and roll after roll; it had become almost a feature of the morning watch on the tail of a gale. With the dawn I saw that high on the leach of the mainsail was a small tear that might spread if not repaired. Down came the mainsail, and as we secured it temporarily with sail tyers the wind fell flat.

Belmore rolled with violent abandon.

The main was again ready within five minutes, and the wind came in with a good puff from west-north-west; it had veered twelve points as the 'low' centre passed overhead. By 8.30 a.m. she was settled with a full main, the R.O.R.C. boomed out to port, and working jib set flying to starboard; wind west-north-west, nineteen knots, confused sea average height eighteen feet. She might have sailed faster under a spinnaker, but I was expecting each minute a gale on the rise of pressure, stronger than the hard blow we had experienced on the fall.

All round were the appearances of fronts that might herald the new gale, and overhead was dull overcast without the rain. I waited for an hour, then secured myself in a soaking berth and tried hopelessly to sleep.

By noon, 16th July, the following wind had lightened from the north-west, and the motion was even more violent with less weight in the sails to steady her. The spinnaker would only add to the rolling, and certainly put her boom ends under the water with the danger of breaking them. The speed had dropped to 6·9 knots, and the steady low reading of the barometer was discouraging until I turned to write up the log for midday, with bearing checks by directional radio. In fourteen hours we had covered 182 miles, most of it from a gale before the beam; it was a staggering achievement for a yacht the size of *Belmore*; with that news some sleep was possible whatever the motion.

That day was *Belmore*'s. Yacht for yacht, no other competitor sailed so far; *Delight*'s lead of fifty-two miles at the previous noon was down to twenty-eight miles, and we had caught up on *Figaro* in Class B. The yachts ahead had still to enjoy the full benefit of that slow-moving gale, which had moderated considerably when it caught them up; even *Delight* at a distance slightly greater from the centre may not have enjoyed quite the bounteous crop of wind that came to *Belmore*.

A superb gale, but even with such fortune an eleven-ton yacht needed a stout crew to seize 182 nautical miles from its ravings.

There followed an uneasy day; the weather held the cards and it would hit again without warning. For twenty hours we remained in the 'low' centre with fitful winds from astern. Then as the barometer began to move up slowly around mid-night the wind moved round to head us from the north-east, but it was not until 0930, with breakfast cleared away, that it again began to blow hard; then came a squall from east-north-east with heavy rain; we shifted straight from C.C.A. to worker jib, and began to fight steadily through the usual succession of changes down; it was a classic forenoon for sail-shifters, which would have been a feat even had the main halyard winch been perfect; seven sail changes were recorded in the log before noon, when she settled under ten rolls and spitfire jib.

The log read at 1230 hours:

Course 110 degrees. Hour's run 6·7 miles. Mean wind N.E. 38 knots. Gale force 8. Sea confused 18 feet. Pounding occasionally. Hard on the gale. Waves sweeping right over deck. Cold.

It had been only a moderate run to noon, with 145 miles sailed mostly in the storm centre, but that low would still give a great deal more wind, even if it were to stick right on the nose. The afternoon shipping forecast gave the centre of the 'low' in *Belmore*'s position, and soon after forecast the warning for our area of a new gale, north-west and backing: severe at times.

'Those met-men astern of station again,' said Tim briskly. 'The rain has already eased and it's blowing less.'

It probably was blowing a trifle less, and at 1630 the log recorded wind down to thirty-knots mean speed, but it was some time before we got any more sail on, as this time the sea was already rough and built up rapidly; the southerly gale had left its swell, then another swell rode over it from the west, and the north-east gale caused a chaotic stir on the top of all that. Then the gale freed three points to north-by-east, causing a slap-up battle of swells and seas in the proper Western Ocean style. Still *Belmore* was being driven at over five knots, hard on the wind; once she was swept from end to end by a green wave from ahead, then a few seconds later pooped by a persistent swell from astern.

The yacht just did not seem to mind what the waves did, and plunged ahead in a way that seemed absurd for so small a craft. The wind had remained steady from north-by-east for two hours, still blowing twenty-eight knots, before I ventured more sail. She increased her speed nearly half a knot and after one or two heavy smacks seemed no more concerned with the seas than she had been before. The barometer was on its way up. So another two rolls came out and the heavy-weather jib took the place of the spitfire on the promise that the gale was definitely moderating.

The next two hours were Tim's watch; two hours on the tiller was too much for one man under those conditions, so between us we drove her 12·3 miles. This had none of the exhilarating run-away thrill of the wave-riding off the wind, it was sheer battering with the grim determination to hold on. It was difficult to steer a course in those conditions as our compass card seemed reluctant to keep up to its work; each time

she crashed into a wave barrier the compass would shy off
and sometimes come back only after a wander of 360 degrees.
Fortunately the low clouds were clearing and this made it
easier to sense the course when the compass lost its head. It
was like two hours of bantam-weights standing up to a heavy-
weight boxer; if the seas had been able to get hold of anything
on the deck of *Belmore* they would have torn it from her and
pounded at the open wound.

Then at 2030, when I was expecting things might get
worse as we sailed on to the Rockall Bank, the seas eased per-
ceptibly; at least two of the underlying swells seemed to have
felt that a fifty-fathom bank was too shallow for their deep
ocean waves. *Belmore* noticed the change and each hour she
speeded up a cable or two, although the wind lost a couple of
knots in the same period. Before midnight we sighted a pair
of trawlers, not fishing but lying a-try on the banks until the
conditions improved. Later another one sighted us and got
under way, steaming towards us to see if we were in trouble;
our only anxiety was that the craft might get anywhere near
us in those conditions, so Mike turned off course to shun
her.

Through the night we sailed on across Rockall Bank with
six rolls in the main and forward the heavy-weather jib set;
not once did she drop below 6·4 knots, hard on the wind, so
we were certainly not laggardly in setting more sail. Below,
sleep cannot be called impossible, because George achieved it
when he was off watch, but no one else managed better than
short periods broken by some change in the violent rhythm of
the motion. We also had to pump each hour, and every part
of the yacht was as soggy as a peat bog.

With trawlers sighted and Rockall estimated twenty miles
off our track, extra care was needed over the look-out,
although even a glance to windward in those conditions was
painful. The trawlers, each time, were sighted in the dark at

least a couple of miles away, but a yacht might well remain unseen at half a mile off or less.

Perhaps one came as close as this to *Belmore* that night, as sometime during the five hours of darkness we overtook *Delight*, hove-to on the same tack.

We knew nothing of this at the time, nor that at noon she was twenty-eight miles astern, after having led us for 2660 miles from Bermuda. At dawn the seas were more regular, but having seen that she would carry no more sail without loss of speed, I tried to dry up some of the bog below. We were safely past Rockall itself, but navigation was still important with our landfall likely within twenty-four hours. Sights were impossible in heavy rain, and radio bearings little use until a chart could be made dry enough to draw pencil lines. I lit the cooking-stove, hooked on the cook's steadying belt round my waist, and, a few square inches at a time, dried out part of the chart over the gas ring. Inside the cabin the temperature was just under fifty degrees, but with a northerly blow it was very much colder outside, so condensed drops dripped even if waves no longer washed over the deck to send jets under the edge of the hatch, or dollops each time it was opened.

I found George's favourite chamois leather and wiped off the moisture from the deckhead; but by the time I had worked forward to the mast beam the drops were as large as ever in the dog-house aft. Everything was wet. I started the whole thing over again, then stopped half-way; here was the gale, the tough gale for which we had prepared for so long, and the best I could do about it was to fuss about in the cabin like a broody old Mrs. Mop. The deck was the place I ought to be, keeping up the offensive, stirring up enthusiasm to race harder.

Reluctantly I dragged on oilskins, then heaved myself up the fore-hatch, as we had not been using the main hatch for twelve hours due to the amount of water it let straight down into the galley. It was still raining, and spray beat over the deck; she could not quite make the course we wanted, but was probably averaging about ten degrees from it. 'There's no point in any more sail until we can ease the sheets,' I said to Mike, then added to myself: 'As it is, I think she's really sailing too fast to be sensible.'

I went below for the 0745 shipping forecast. There were gale warnings for our area and many others to the east and south, but annoyingly there was none for Orkney, where I expected the leading yachts of Class B to be about that time. The storm-centre was still reported to be near us, moving east-north-east and filling slowly; for Rockall area the gales would die, with wind backing to the north-west. 'Splendid,' I thought. 'Good running conditions, weather clearing, an odd sun-sight this morning, clothes hung on deck to dry this afternoon; star-sights this evening. All perfect for a good land-fall tomorrow morning on the Flannan Isles; perhaps even the Butt of Lewis a bit later if the visibility is not too good.'

Yet by 0800 the rain was heavier. 'Wind freshening, I think,' said Mike, opening the hatch for a second. Then I noticed that the barometer had stopped its upward climb. I could see only one explanation after that radio forecast: we were sailing as fast as the depression and perhaps getting even a trifle nearer the centre once more.

'Going to moderate, sir?' asked Barry, when he saw my dictated shipping forecast on the chart-table.

'Probably not yet,' I answered. 'This may hold up until the afternoon.'

'No, oh no,' said Roy, putting aside breakfast which Barry had prepared punctually in spite of the weather. 'Not more. We've had quite enough.'

'You might just as well eat your breakfast before it spills,' suggested Barry.

Turning over the watch took a long time in that weather and it was nearing 9 a.m. when Mike slumped down the fore-hatch on to the wet sails. He lay there too exhausted to take off his oilskins for some minutes, and then took little interest in breakfast. I offered him a warming tot, but he declined it. Still uppermost in my mind was the easing after the blow, and always it had been my plan to have Mike on the fore-deck hanking on bigger genoas; if he was as tired as this none of us would have the strength to force on sail. There were some sleeping-pills in my locker, and they had proved fairly strong when used for easing down after the race in Bermuda; I found a couple and put them in Mike's cup of coffee; his mouth would be too full of salt water to taste them, and I did not want to waste effort arguing about it. Mike needed some real sleep if he was to take this leading part several hours ahead.

The pills worked well, and Mike was soon fast asleep; if I took his two-hour watch from 1030 to 1230 there would be no more need for him until 1630, and I felt it was likely that the blow would continue until then. In my watch there was a slight freshening, although the rain stopped and she actually speeded up to log 13·9 miles in the two hours; it was impressive the way *Belmore* sailed into the great seas, but rather awesome at times to see big ones charging down on her from to windward.

Within a few minutes under these conditions the mind was dulled; there was the compass card, the sails, and the waves to windward. All else was lost.

A wave piling to windward might seem due to break just as it reached us, but she had ample speed for a heave on the tiller in good time to let her swerve clear to leeward of the curling cataract.

At first I regularly searched the whole arc of bearings every few minutes, turning in the deep cockpit to sweep my eyes through the weather quarter behind me, and pausing each time she dropped in the trough of a wave; but nearly every time I turned round for this careful look-out search the reward was a heavy slap from a wave that curled over her unnoticed. Soon I gave up the look-out astern and was content to watch only the sea to windward, the tiny area of sails, and the compass card.

It was when I went below again I noticed the shriek in

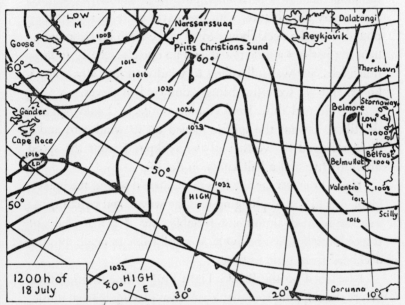

FIG. 4. The *Belmore* still 'hooked on to' the low

the rigging had pitched higher as it fought with a gale. She was soon dragging the feet of the sails through the water, and there was nothing for it but another change down; first we went down to the spitfire jib whose high-cut foot keeps it clear of the water, but a couple of hours later waves were sweeping right over the yacht once more, and we took in a couple more rolls in the main.

'So much for easing and backing to north-west,' I said as

we came below. 'It hasn't moved a quarter point from north-by-east, and now it's blowing force eight.'

'I'll tell them. I'll bloddy well tell them, if we get home.' George was getting quite angry. 'I'll see no one volunteers for one of these larks again. This is bloddy hell.'

'Tea or coffee, George?' asked Barry.

Whether it was just the sea and the gale, or whether it was the judgement of a tired man, but things seemed worse then than at any time before, with the waves more vicious as they pounded on the deck above. Mike woke from his sleep indignant but perhaps a little rested, and no one else seemed to have much left. She was still sailing to windward into a gale at six knots, and we were just being hammered to pieces.

'Second and third hand coming on deck,' I told Mike at the tiller. 'I want the spitfire hauled up to windward and a dodger rigged to weather of the cockpit. I want the speed down to five and a half knots on the log.'

Half a knot less speed felt as though we'd put on the brakes. Gone was that wild plunging into the waves, and by comparison she seemed almost comfortable; but if a man did not secure himself down below he was still liable to crack into the deckhead from time to time.

I switched on the B.B.C. Light Programme in good time before the shipping forecast; a band was playing martial music, so I tuned the set loud to know without earphones when the music ceased; it could be heard in the cabin even through the howls of the gale and the rush of the waves. Then as the music ceased I quickly put on the earphones.

'That was the band of the Royal Marine School of Music,' I told George, a Royal Marine of many years' service.

His eyes lit up with pride; that band playing at a seaside town in the south of England gave us many miles during George's long night watch which came soon afterwards.

Fifty minutes after the shipping forecast, which foretold

numerous gales, but winds backing to the north-west in our area, the wind-shriek in the rigging came down half an octave in its tune; the barometer had started up again. 'What do you think now?' I asked Mike on the tiller.

'I think it's still increasing,' he answered.

'You can never tell up there,' I told him. 'There's too much ruddy wind in the cockpit to know what the weather's doing. We'll let fly that spitfire and sail on.'

She took it all right, and Mike seemed to feel he must not be outdone. 'I want to change up, sir. Heavy-weather jib and a couple of rolls out.'

She took that too and whacked up the speed for the next hour to seven knots; apparently sailing about sixty degrees from the wind.

'I believe you have been steering off, Mike,' I suggested when he came below. 'How could a yacht do seven knots to windward into a gale?'

'Perhaps I let her off a trifle sometimes,' he answered, 'but I like to keep moving.'

During the first night watch the wind actually increased again, and George suggested a change down to spitfire jib. 'She must stick it out,' I answered without going on deck. 'If a sail blows out I'll just have to buy the owner a new one.'

By then I was tuned to navigation, and could face no more sail-shifts down. Etched on my mind was the need to keep strength for that much rehearsed piling on of sails as a grand finale to conclude the storm.

Navigation was an ample cause of worry during the five hours of darkness; had the weather been clear the northern summer night would scarcely have become dark at all, but under the dense cloud-layers of the gale visibility through rain and spray was probably less than a mile. I had taken no star-sights for the nine days since 9th July, having thrown away the last chance on the evening of 14th July when I elected to

'He calls that a beard!' Mike Tanner and Tim Sex

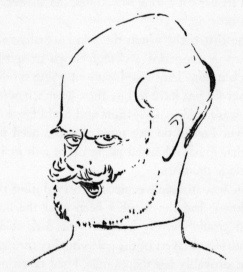

"Who wants to grow hair on his chin
anyway?"—Barry

'Want some of mine?'
Roy Mullender and George Wheatley

'Of course . . . if you chaps *must* look like
tramps!'—The skipper

put seamanship before navigation, with the false hopes of many good stars to come; there had been no clear view of the sun since that same 14th July when several positional lines had been plotted. An uncertain position-line had been gained the previous morning, south of Rockall, from a glimpse of the sun's outline seen through cloud; in rough seas and doubtful visibility such sight-taking was an erratic gamble.

Knowledge of our position therefore depended mostly on radio reception of Consol; these bearings are notoriously unreliable in the dark hours, and the more so when the beam travels over high land. The signal that mattered most for our landfall came from Stavangar in Norway over the tops of the Scottish Highlands.

Our track, judged by these uncertain aids, aimed straight for a landfall on the Flannan Islands, which by my estimate we could not reach before noon next day at the earliest. But if we were only fifteen miles to leeward of this track we could sail into the sheer face of St. Kilda, mounting up from the Atlantic depths to a 1000-foot-high cliff, which made a lee shore to the northerly gale; the island had no lighthouse and was not inhabited. The particularly high speed logged during the dog watches made me feel that the Consol bearing was at fault and we had run off to leeward from the supposed course hard on the wind.

So long as it was dark I stayed impatiently at the charttable, frequently checking the Consol count and anxiously alert for any sign of land nearby; there was little point in remaining on deck to add to the look-out of the watch. Up there wind, spray, and rain soon battered the senses to a dull insensitivity, and there was a better chance down below to notice that change in the pattern of the sea which must come when waves are reflected back from a cliff face. There might also be a change of wind near such steep land, and perhaps even a dead area close in under the cliff; once there the waves would carry a small yacht with them where her anchor cable could not reach the bottom and her sails could not carry her clear. Soundings would give no warning as our equipment was not intended to measure such deep water. We depended for safety on our senses, and anxious alertness has a large appetite of nervous energy.

The change of the watches at 0230 brought me some relief; men fresh on watch, even coming from the abominable conditions of that cold, wet, hurtling cabin, have alerter senses than men at the end of six hard hours on deck. 'Thank God I had that cockpit dodger rigged last night,' I thought.

'Try not to let her run off,' I told Mike as he prepared to go on deck. 'Only an hour until first light, and we must keep up to 080 on the compass.'

The chance of a premature landfall in the dark was so much on my own mind that it did not occur to me in that befuddled state of exhaustion that he did not know all about it too.

'Thirty-eight point two miles in your six hours, George,' I mentioned as he came below. 'That's 6·4 knots. Could she sail any closer than 080?'

'Not unless you reduce sail, sir. She's got too ruddy much, I reckon.'

Roy, who had been on watch with George, sat on the lee-cabin berth inflating his rubber lifebelt worn beneath his oilskins.

'Going swimming, Roy?' I asked.

'No, sir. But it makes a good fender when I get bounced about in my sleep; sort of pneumatic body pillow.'

It was a long hour before the first signs of dawn strained into the chart space below.

'All well?' I asked Mike up the hatch.

'Rain's almost stopped, sir. No change in the wind, and we've got nearly seven knots on the clock.'

Too tired to take off oilskins I slumped back into the sodden quarter berth and slept.

It was probably two hours later that Mike came down below. 'The sky is clearing, sir,' he suggested. 'I think you could get the sun's outline already.'

'It's too low,' I excused myself; 'the exact position does not matter all that much now.' Really I knew that I would be unable to work out a sight.

'It won't be long before we might be able to change up,' suggested Mike. 'Would you come and see if you think it's possible?'

'Could she go any faster?' I retaliated.

'Not yet, I suppose, she's still near seven on the clock.'

It was just then that Tim shouted out excitedly: 'There's a bloody great something on the lee bow. Must be land. About five miles away.'

'Oh yes,' I said, still not roused from my stupor even by a landfall after nearly 3000 miles at sea. 'St. Kilda is high.' I was too gale-battered to feel any excitement at the sight of land, or to bother that it was not a very good landfall, some twelve miles to leeward of our track.

'But is it St. Kilda?' asked Mike, who had climbed on deck as soon as Tim reported. 'I thought we expected the Flannan Isles; you never said anything about St. Kilda at the turn-over, sir.'

'How stupid of me,' I answered. 'I forgot.'

Slowly I dragged myself out of the quarter berth to go on deck for a look; still on my way to the deck Mike shouted, almost with glee: 'She dropped point two on the speed log while I was below; wind's easing. Isn't it time to pile on?'

What the landfall could not do the suggestion of piling on sail achieved. 'Pile on as soon as it starts to ease' had been drummed into my mind; it was a habit that now needed no more conscious thought. The catch-words 'time to pile on' acted as a catylist to the last reserves of effort.

'Right,' I answered, 'I'll take her. Two rolls out first and then shift to worker.'

The two of them, Mike and Tim, hurled themselves at the sails like tigers. Barry had passed up the sail-bag from below and was bagging the soaking heavy-weather before coming up to join us on deck. This was it; it was the time to which all our training had aimed, but however hard the training I had never suspected that the gale would be so protracted and the test so severe.

'It's worked; it's come out right,' I told myself.

This release of last reserves of my energy also filtered into my thinking brain, as well as my mainspring of sheer habit. I noticed that my tiller hand was shaking and my sight of the cliffs in the damp air was not too clear.

'Hell!' I said, and Mike turned aft thinking that I'd seen some false lead in the sheets. It was not that; it was the realization that between us we were unfit to sail the yacht close to windward of St. Kilda. 'Ready about, Mike, I'm going to stand out north to get more sea-room.'

Perhaps I felt vaguely the storm was trying subtlety as it died. We had won the first trick with the twenty-four hours of southerly gale as the glass fell; then came the thirty hours of anxious uneasiness in the storm centre, when light westerlies tempted us to relax our guard before the storm struck again with a sudden squall which grew into a gale from the north-east; this had persisted for forty hours, attacking again and again with gusts, squalls, and vicious seas. Was it the storm's final trick to lull us in broad daylight under the cliffs of St. Kilda for destruction by calms where the blustering gales had failed to deflect this tiny vessel from her purpose? If the wind dropped dead after the storm, when the yacht was scarcely a mile to the north of St. Kilda or its jagged neighbour

Boreray, we could do nothing to prevent the waves left over from driving us helplessly on to an unclimbable rock-race. *Belmore* had no engine; she could not withdraw from the fight even if I wanted.

So we tacked to the north, and as *Belmore* gained sea-room Mike, Tim, and Barry went through the whole process of piling on, with the speed log never dropping below six knots. The wind eased quickly, but would not relent a point in direction; by the change of the watches at 0830 she was under full mainsail and C.C.A. genoa. With eight miles of sea-room we had tacked back to the eastwards; the Hebrides coast was only fifty miles ahead, so we were now coasting.

The ocean passage was over. Six of us had sailed *Belmore* from Bermuda to St. Kilda in eighteen days sixteen hours. It was 2780 miles, at an average speed of 6·1 knots.

13

St. Kilda to the Skaw

THE ocean passage was finished, the gales were past, but there were still 600 miles to sail. *Escapade* had crossed the finishing line off the tip of Denmark in a half-gale before we sighted St. Kilda, but we were going to beat her on handicap allowance by thirteen and a half hours. *Figaro* finished in fading airs on the evening of 19th July as *Belmore* sailed past the Butt of Lewis; after allowing for handicap she was still to beat us by a day and nearly sixteen hours. Between these two yachts five more of Class A and *Carina* in Class B finished the course, while the rest of these classes were less than a day after *Figaro*.

The deep depression near Rockall, with which the small yachts of Class C had lived for four days, had less influence on the race of the larger classes. When *Belmore* was fighting it out with *Delight* and *Casella* in the northerly gale of 18th July, many of the larger yachts were struggling within sight of each other and the Norwegian coast in light airs; at noon on the 17th July *Figaro* was near Sule Skerry, whose weather station reported the wind as east eighteen knots. It had been an ocean storm, and at no time during the life of the depression did Cape Wrath report a gale, although high winds and big seas were recorded in the ocean station ships in the Atlantic; its influence reached far to the southwards, with a moderate gale recorded at Plymouth and dense rain as the quadruple fronts which it generated, crossed southern England and on up the Continent of Europe.

The depression with its series of gales was the special feature of the small-class race; perhaps *Danegeld* missed its main force. When the gale of 15th July was giving *Belmore* her best day's run of 182 miles, *Danegeld*, 246 miles to the south-west, was outside the area of a strong blow; during the next four days she caught up to 130 miles away on 19th July, but the synoptic charts suggested for her track no more than a brisk half-gale; but it is hard to feel her crew were quite serious when they reported after the finish that they had scarcely a dollop of spray on deck and only an occasional shower.

For the crew of *Belmore* the race was chiefly a contest with *Delight* and with *Casella*, as had been planned; it was a battle with Atlantic gales, as had been planned too. Had the start been a trifle sooner or a day later she would have met quite different weather; she might have gone ahead of those gales, as did *Escapade*, or have come in behind them as did *Danegeld*. Such are the chances of the Western Ocean.

Delight led the small class for seventeen days. In the early stages of the race she pressed harder than *Belmore* and gained distance beyond her handicap allowance, so that at one time she was perhaps the best-placed in all the fleet. But her effort cost her equipment, and perhaps crew strength as well; a halyard block carried away before she reached Point Able; a spinnaker blew out, and she sailed over it. She had other breakages and her reserves of equipment, and perhaps of crew energy too, were reduced. Had she encountered no worse weather than some other yachts in the race they would have been sufficient, but she chanced to get the conditions that we in *Belmore* had prayed for; that was my good luck. On 14th July *Delight* was forty-four miles ahead of *Belmore*; on 19th July she was twenty-eight miles astern.

We could know nothing of this as we sailed quietly up the

coast of the Hebrides on the afternoon of 19th July, delighting in a watery beam of sunshine that made barren Flannan Islands seem like a green pasture.

'How do you think we're doing, sir?' asked Roy.

'It is pure guesswork about the big ones,' I answered, 'but I don't think they have finished yet. Assuming we all had similar weather we haven't lost many miles yet. Had the D.R. been ten miles closer to St. Kilda, or the gale gone on an hour or two longer, I might have hove-to, but we just kept going.'

'What about our own class?' asked Barry.

'I'm quite certain we're in the lead. No one in their senses would have kept a small yacht hammering into those gales so long; it would leave the crew too gale-battered on making the land, even if it did not smash up the yacht herself.'

'But that's just what you did, sir,' said Roy.

'Yes, I suppose we did.'

'Well, I wouldn't mind having another crack,' said George.

Before midnight we crept quietly round the Butt of Lewis and turned eastwards for North Ronaldshay in Orkney. The wind was light, still from the north, and the swell no more than enough to give her a sleepy roll. Off watch we slept, still wet and cold.

The morning of 20th July was cloudless and sunshine warm; then the wind crawled round astern so that the spinnaker boom made another spar on which to hang bedding, clothes, and charts. For me, nostalgia hung sweet and sticky to my thoughts; there were the mountains of Sutherland, then Orkney's Hoy Hill, Rora Head, and the Old Man of Hoy; these were places I knew well after living two happy years in the Island of Hoy. Never had they looked more beautiful as the sun shone on a pleasant land after so many days of driving cloud and gale-shattered ocean.

In spite of the quiet seas and warm sunshine our nerves were still jagged and torn. It was like flattened batteries put on charge, as the first ill-shapen bubbles form in uneven patterns on the plates; the re-charging of nervous energy after complete exhaustion was a painful process. A tot of whisky helped to lubricate the charging pains between different cells of the battery that formed the crew.

Sails were torn as well as nerves frayed. Our mainsail of twelve-ounce terylene, made new for this venture, had to be lowered for the third time to repair split seams; either the edges of the needle-holes were sharp or it may be that the threads do not sink into the material as with cotton sails.

At midnight the breeze freshened, but against all advice from the shipping forecasts it insisted on veering to the southeast. We forced past North Ronaldshay at good speed against the strong tide, but this and the head wind shoved us up northwards; so with the early morning we skimmed heeling past the southern tip of Fair Island.

The breeze soon lightened, but all day and the next it persisted from an easterly direction. It was thwarting to tack to windward against light airs, and worse still through those hours when *Belmore* lay becalmed; but *Delight*, at least, should be suffering as much as us. On Saturday, 23rd July, *Belmore* logged only 60·1 miles, and *Delight*, which has passed north of Fair Island, got back into the lead; *Danegeld* that day logged almost twice our run to recover her loss of the previous day, when *Belmore* was welcomed into the North Sea with a run of only eighty-three miles.

At last the wind came into the north-west to fulfil Met. prophecies which had been repeated for day after day without result. In *Belmore* we steered well south of the Norwegian coast, along which a west-going current sets out of the Baltic; we searched for the counter-current that creeps down the Danish coast. This tactic paid off and we ran quietly under spinnaker up the Skagerrak through Sunday, 24th July. The sun was bright, the sky was blue, with scattered trawlers dotting the calm sea; each time a new sail was sighted I hurried up the mast with binoculars, searching for some rival yacht, but all were the steadying sails of trawlers. The nearest yacht ahead had finished three days before us, while *Casella* was twenty miles astern and *Delight* twice that distance.

Close in, we passed Danish hamlets on the coast. Then as the sun set a red light blinked ahead.

It was the Skaw Light Vessel.

We turned after crossing the line and beat back against the freshening breeze to ask the result.

'You are the winners,' came from the lightship in English.

'What of?' asked Tim, whose voice was good for long-range hailing at sea.

'Of Class C,' came the answer. 'You are the first of the class to finish.'

'*Danegeld* still has five hours to beat us,' someone suggested. 'But I wonder how the other classes did?'

For the moment I had no more wonders; George took charge for a quiet five-hour sail to Marstand, unhampered by spinnakers and large genoas, while I enjoyed my longest sleep for twenty-five days and nights.

14

Home Again

O UR night-time arrival in the quiet summer resort of Marstand was almost tumultuous. Although it was three o'clock in the morning, a large crowd gathered on the wharf where *Belmore* secured by her bows, an assortment of musical instruments joined to play 'Rule Britannia', an attractive Swedish girl came onboard to present a bunch of flowers, followed by the sailing committee, and a gang of fellow crewmen from the larger yachts who brought fresh fruit, rum, and a crate of beer.

In the afternoon we were told: 'When we see the King of Norway sail in at the end of his race today two guns will be fired. That means the prize-giving will be held in half an hour.'

The guns fired, and in time a royal prize-giving was added to the princely welcome of the middle watch. For winning the smallest class the cup was the biggest of all.

Then off to sea for a voyage of 750 miles back to England. Much of the time the wind was very light, and sometimes we lay becalmed for hour after hour in the North Sea or close off the low coasts of Holland and Belgium; even in the English Channel the calms persisted, when one evening we watched the sun set over Hastings and saw it rise again over Beachy Head. The quiet weather gave us a chance to scrape off the remains of topside bright-work and renew the varnish on the rail and the boom.

Those nine days of quiet cruising at sea, as long as it had taken us to sail half-way across from Bermuda to Scotland, gave ample scope, too, to discuss our races. The results in themselves gave ample satisfaction. No other yacht had gained a class place in both Bermuda and Transatlantic races; in no other class had the Transatlantic race been won by such a wide margin as the eleven hours thirty-two minutes that separated *Belmore* from her runner-up.

But how could we have done better? What could be improved? How did the scheme work out? Had such rigid discipline and elaborate preparation been necessary?

The races of *Belmore* for the Royal Naval Sailing Association had been so much my plan, my method, and my execution that I am myself a partial judge. Better perhaps to quote on these points from an article published by Mike Tanner a month or two after the races:

One of my main impressions after the races had finished was surprise how we all came through the physical and mental strain without all of us snapping each other's heads off.

Behind this impression of surprise is really the crux of why we did so well in the races and were able to live amicably together for three months of intense training and racing in confined and often uncomfortable conditions.

Careful and rigid training, with extreme attention to the minutest detail, enabled the skipper to weld us into a happy and efficient crew. As a result we were able to do far more than we ever previously have thought ourselves capable of doing.

This state of training was achieved by intensive sail drills, repeating them over and over again until we cut down the time taken to the minimum, whilst at the same time avoiding the chances of accidents. This state was also helped by the fact that each member of the crew had a certain department to look after. This fostered keen rivalry between us to ensure that one's own department was always at first readiness to meet any requirement, and nothing was missing when needed.

This method of training enabled us to find out early each other's idiosyncrasies and put up with them; it resulted in us coming to the starting line almost at the peak of our form, although we were unfortunate to have to make a crew change, due to an accident, just prior to the Bermuda race.

My chief memories of the race were not so much of the wet and discomfort, but of the tiredness and exasperation during the calm periods. I felt that I was pretty fit at the start of both races, but concentration on steering well, and constant sail changing, made me far more tired than I thought I ever would be. Sound sleep is very difficult in bad weather and my general level of tiredness was brought home to me after the skipper had given me sleeping pills without my knowledge, and I slept soundly for seven hours. During the calms after gales I got very irritated and exasperated, particularly so in light airs as it is such hard work keeping the yacht sailing as fast as she should be.

Looking back, several points stand out where we could have done better; better helmsmanship, better sail trimming and better concentration by night; most of this means more experience. Our diet needed more fresh food, and physical health at times caused worries. Our day-to-day watch-keeping routine worked very well, but I think it was a pity that through accident we had to combine the duties of skipper and navigator, as each seemed a heavy job.

That was the opinion of Mike Tanner, youngest man of the crew, but one who had much previous experience of ocean racing. His expression 'we were able to do far more than we ever previously thought ourselves capable of doing' is significant. Perhaps the real attraction of such hard ocean racing is in finding new qualities, new powers of endurance, and new tolerance to human trial.

It was misty as on 5th August we crept past the Owers light-ship with the last of the afternoon ebb. Then a breeze stirred and a warship steamed up towards us from the Nab. By the time we reached Spithead, towed in over the floodtide, *Belmore* was surrounded by an escort of several craft. Off

Portsmouth we slipped the tow for the satisfaction of sailing into harbour.

Soon after 5 p.m. the sails were lowered for the last time of our venture; as the genoa was gathered on deck *Belmore* glided quietly between the two groups of moored warships. This time she was inward bound, and since sailing outwards between them she had covered afloat more than 6000 miles, part ocean and partly through the waters of ten different countries. It would have been satisfactory if we could have hoisted the signal 'Evolution completed' at the yard-arm, but my orders had not been fully executed. We were home well within the limit set and the yacht was in need of no repair; but the instructions from my commodore were to win in each race. Certainly we had won our class in the Transatlantic, but in the Bermuda race it was only a second, so her yard-arms were bare as *Belmore* carried her way gently to the captain's gangway of H.M.S. *Vernon*.

The burgee of the Royal Naval Sailing Association fluttered proudly from the masthead.

Appendix I

Year and Race (Approx. length in miles)	Yacht (Length overall)	Skipper (Nationality)	Days Elapsed
1866 Sandy Hook to Needles (3100)	*Henrietta* (107)	Capt. Samuels (American)	13
1870 Ireland to Sandy Hook (2900)	*Cambria* (108)	Capt. Tannock (British)	23
1877 New York to Ireland (2900)	*Coronet* (133)	Capt. Crosby (American)	15
1891 Boston to Lizard (2700) (Single-handed)	*Sea Serpent* (15)	S. Lawlor (American)	45
1905 Sandy Hook to Lizard (3000)	*Atlantic* (185)	Capt. C. Barr (American)	12
1928 New York to Santander (3300) Large Class	*Elena* (137)	Capt. J. Barr (American)	17
Small Class	*Nina* (59)	Paul Hammond (American)	24
1931 Newport to Plymouth (2800)	*Dorade* (52)	Olin Stephens (American)	17
1935 Newport to Bergen (3100)	*Stormy Weather* (53)	Rod Stephens (American)	19

Year and Race (Approx. length in miles)	Yacht (Length overall)	Skipper (Nationality)	Days Elapsed
1936 Bermuda to Cuxhaven (3400)	Roland von Bremen (59)	Dr. Franz Perlia (German)	21
1950 Bermuda to Plymouth (2900)	Cohoe (32)	Adlard Coles (British)	21
1952 Bermuda to Plymouth (2900)			
Large Class	Caribbee (58)	Carleton Mitchell (American)	21
Small Class	Samuel Pepys (30)	Erroll Bruce (British)	25
1955 Newport to Marstand (3400)	Carina (53)	Richard Nye (American)	20
1957 Newport to Santander (3100)			
Large Class	Carina	Richard Nye	18
Small Class	White Mist (46)	Blunt White (American)	19
1960 Plymouth to New York (3100) (Single-handed)	Gipsy Moth (39)	Francis Chichester (British)	40
1960 Bermuda to Marstand (3500)			
Large Class	Ondine (58)	S. A. Long (American)	20
Medium Class	Figaro (47)	William Snaith (American)	20
Small Class	Belmore (36)	Erroll Bruce (British)	24

Appendix II

SAILS USED IN THE BERMUDA AND
TRANSATLANTIC RACES

Name	Area	Material	Remarks
Old main	316 sq. ft.	10 oz. terylene	Reserve sail only
New main	316 sq. ft.	12 oz. terylene	Normal mainsail
Trysail	110 sq. ft.	12 oz. cotton	
C.C.A. genoa	460 sq. ft.	7 oz. terylene	Cruising Club of America rule
Ghoster	386 sq. ft.	$3\frac{1}{2}$ oz. terylene	
R.O.R.C. genoa	365 sq. ft.	7 oz. terylene	Royal Ocean Racing Club limit
Working jib	290 sq. ft.	10 oz. terylene	
Heavy-weather jib	135 sq. ft.	12 oz. cotton	
Spitfire jib	60 sq. ft.	10 oz. cotton	
Heavy spinnaker		$2\frac{1}{2}$ oz. nylon	
Light spinnaker		$1\frac{1}{2}$ oz. terylene	
Storm spinnaker		$2\frac{1}{2}$ oz. terylene	
Spinnaker staysail		$3\frac{1}{2}$ oz. terylene	

Index